Jaime Sucher

Golden
Retrievers

Everything about Feeding,
Health Care, Training, Grooming,
Exercise, and Play Activities

BARRON'S

2 CONTENTS

3

SHOULD YOU BUY A GOLDEN RETRIEVER?

There is little wonder as to why the Golden Retriever has become one of the most popular purebred dogs in America. They are loyal, intelligent, well-behaved, gentle, and eager to please—and that is just scratching the surface.

The "Perfect" Dog

The popularity of the Golden Retriever, to an extent, is very much a reflection of our modern society's concept of the perfect family dog. It is a very attractive breed that requires a minimum of grooming to keep it in "show" condition. Goldens are reasonably clean, and they are very easy to maintain in top physical and mental health. The breed has been shown to be tremendously versatile, as Goldens are proven Seeing Eye dogs and are also used by authorities to search out explosives and narcotics. They also possess the ideal temperament for a family dog.

Goldens are "people" dogs. They are a friendly, gentle, and eager breed that truly need human companionship. Anyone who takes the time and effort to establish a positive rapport with a Golden will be rewarded with a loving and affectionate friend that will do anything to please his master.

Goldens are easy to train, because they really love to learn. Their favorite time may well be the training session. This breed has the ability to learn practically anything a human can teach a dog to do. This trait has made them a popular hunting dog, as well as a dominant force in the obedience ring.

Although these qualities may be found in all Goldens, the owner must be sure they are developed and become part of the dog's personality. Bringing out the best in your dog will take time, energy, patience, and understanding.

Important Note: To buy, or not to buy, a Golden Retriever is an important decision. Many people who purchase dogs are not aware of all the responsibilities of dog ownership at four-legged companion imaginable. However, if your puppy is given little training, he may grow up to be eighty pounds of unruly hyperactivity— a situation that no dog owner could cope with for very long.

Therefore, selecting an adult Golden also offers advantages. A well-trained adult makes a marvelous pet. He can save you the time and effort needed for rearing and training a puppy. Mature Goldens almost always adapt easily to new owners and environments. A housebroken, trained adult Golden makes an ideal companion for owners for whom raising puppies may be too much work. The greatest drawback to buying an older Golden is that you may find it extremely difficult to correct any bad habits the dog has already acquired.

When choosing between a Golden puppy and an adult, keep in mind that raising a puppy will allow you to train him to the habits of your home. Adult dogs, on the other hand, need significantly less attention, which means less work and effort, especially for an older owner.

Ownership Options

If you are looking for a show dog, you have two options. First, you can purchase a potential show puppy from a reputable breeder and raise him yourself. This way you will have the satisfaction of knowing that you have done the job yourself. If you do not need this satisfaction, you can purchase a mature show dog; this way you are assured of your Golden's quality and beauty.

Whether you choose a puppy or an adult is an extremely important decision. However, the choice of the sex of the dog is not always as important. Golden females (bitches) are just as good a choice as males. Females are usually only slightly smaller and lighter than males.

In addition, there is no significant difference in temperament between the sexes.

The only time you might prefer a specific sex is if you are interested in breeding the dog. If you are considering starting a kennel, females are preferable. If you select a female and have no intention of breeding her, have the dog neutered. Because there are an alarming number of homeless dogs in the United States, owners should take all possible precautions against the needless proliferation of unwanted animals. Another advantage of neutering is avoiding the messiness that will occur when she is "in heat." The female will also be more likely to avoid breast tumors, ovarian cysts, false pregnancies, and other ailments if she has been neutered.

Note that if you plan to enter your female in a dog show, she will be disqualified if she is neutered. A neutered dog, however, may compete in field and obedience trials.

Selecting the Right Puppy for You

If you wish to buy a high-quality Golden, it is of utmost importance that you deal with a well-established and reputable source. You can get a list of reliable Golden Retriever breeders in your area from the American Kennel Club (AKC), the secretary of the GRCA, or your local Golden club. You can also perform a Web search for Golden breeders, but you should never buy a dog online, as the Internet is full of people who would not hesitate to mislead and take advantage of unwary buyers. Instead, use the Internet to find breeders to add to your list of kennels to visit. Also keep in mind that while it may be more convenient to obtain a Golden from a local breeder, traveling the

✔ Do you have a large yard, or is there a park or woods nearby where your dog can get his much-needed exercise? A Golden is a remarkable breed and can adapt to any living quarters that can sensibly house a medium-large breed. However, because the Golden is bred for hunting, exercise is an important part of his physical and mental well-being.

✔ Finally, can you afford to keep a Golden Retriever? Aside from the initial expenses of buying the dog and purchasing necessary supplies, the cost of feeding may be expensive. And don't forget additional expenses such as annual visits to the veterinarian.

You should consider these questions carefully before you buy a Golden Retriever. Find out if there is a chapter of the Golden Retriever Club of America (GRCA) in your area. This organiza-tion can help answer any questions you may have. Remember, owning a dog of any breed is a serious responsibility. If you do not care for the dog properly, his health and happiness will suffer, and you will not experience the pleasure and satisfaction of raising a Golden Retriever.

An Adult or a Puppy?

The Rewards of Ownership

One of the great rewards of owning a Golden Retriever is watching him grow from an awkward, tiny bundle of fur into a thoroughly trained, well-behaved, beautiful adult. However, this requires a great deal of patience, time, and energy. If you work diligently with your puppy during the early training phases, you will be rewarded with the most loving four-legged companion imaginable. However, if your puppy is given little training, he may grow up to be eighty pounds of unruly hyperactivity—a situation that no dog owner could cope with for very long.

Therefore, selecting an adult Golden also offers advantages. A well-trained adult makes a marvelous pet. He can save you the time and effort needed for rearing and training a puppy. Mature Goldens almost always adapt easily to new owners and environments. A housebroken, trained adult Golden makes an ideal companion for owners for whom raising puppies may be too much work. The greatest drawback to buying an older Golden is that you may find it extremely difficult to correct any bad habits the dog has already acquired.

When choosing between a Golden puppy and an adult, keep in mind that raising a puppy will allow you to train him to the habits of your home. Adult dogs, on the other hand, need significantly less attention, which means less work and effort, especially for an older owner.

Ownership Options

If you are looking for a show dog, you have two options. First, you can purchase a potential show puppy from a reputable breeder and raise him yourself. This way you will have the satisfaction of knowing that you have done the job yourself. If you do not need this satisfaction, you can purchase a mature show dog; this way you are assured of your Golden's quality and beauty.

Whether you choose a puppy or an adult is an extremely important decision. However, the choice of the sex of the dog is not always as important. Golden females (bitches) are just as good a choice as males. Females are usually only slightly smaller and lighter than males.

In addition, there is no significant difference in temperament between the sexes.

The only time you might prefer a specific sex is if you are interested in breeding the dog. If you are considering starting a kennel, females are preferable. If you select a female and have no intention of breeding her, have the dog neutered. Because there are an alarming number of homeless dogs in the United States, owners should take all possible precautions against the needless proliferation of unwanted animals. Another advantage of neutering is avoiding the messiness that will occur when she is "in heat." The female will also be more likely to avoid breast tumors, ovarian cysts, false pregnancies, and other ailments if she has been neutered.

Note that if you plan to enter your female in a dog show, she will be disqualified if she is neutered. A neutered dog, however, may compete in field and obedience trials.

Selecting the Right Puppy for You

If you wish to buy a high-quality Golden, it is of utmost importance that you deal with a well-established and reputable source. You can get a list of reliable Golden Retriever breeders in your area from the American Kennel Club (AKC), the secretary of the GRCA, or your local Golden club. You can also perform a Web search for Golden breeders, but you should never buy a dog online, as the Internet is full of people who would not hesitate to mislead and take advantage of unwary buyers. Instead, use the Internet to find breeders to add to your list of kennels to visit. Also keep in mind that while it may be more convenient to obtain a Golden from a local breeder, traveling the extra distance to visit as many breeders as possible is sometimes worth it.

Make appointments with all of the breeders on your list. During your visit, be sure to inspect both the dogs and their housing. Make sure the facilities are clean and spacious, and that the adult dogs are happy and appear healthy. Pay attention to all of the following factors.

✔ Above all, a Golden must be healthy and possess a temperament typical of the breed. When you first look at a puppy, you will see only an adorable energetic bundle of fur and wrinkles. Learn to see past this, and resist the impulse to buy the first puppy that catches your fancy. Examine the puppy's coat; it should be smooth and shiny. His eyes should be bright and have a friendly and curious expression. He should be solidly built. Remember also that Goldens are very people-oriented, and this should be obvious even at an early age. Look for an eager, alert puppy with a wagging tail, and avoid both hyperactive and overly sedate dogs.

✔ Another good indicator of the puppy's temperament is his mother's behavior. After all, many of the puppy's behavioral characteristics are inherited from his sire (father) or dam (mother). Observe how the mother reacts to people. She should be friendly and show no signs of fear or apprehension.

✔ If the puppy appears to be in good health and of sound temperament, the next step is to check the pedigree of his breeding stock. Ask if his medical history is in the Canine Health Information Center (CHIC) database. CHIC is jointly sponsored by the AKC and the Orthopedic Foundation for Animals (OFA). Its goal is to provide a source of information for owners, breeders, and scientists to assist in the breeding of healthy dogs. The CHIC database for Goldens currently includes results of eye clearance tests by the Canine Eye Registry Foundation (CERF), the results of OFA and other veterinary orthopedic group tests for hip and elbow dysplasia, and OFA evaluations for congenital heart defects. CHIC is also working

with the GRCA on creating a DNA database for Goldens, which they hope will lead to the discovery of the genetic links for other canine hereditary ailments. If the breeder does have his or her dogs listed, the results can be reviewed online at *www.caninehealthinfo.org*. If the breeder does not have the dog's test results in the database, you should ask why.

✔ If the dog's pedigree is satisfactory, ask for the date the puppy was wormed and vaccinated, and be sure to get a written record of this for later use by your veterinarian. Do not be afraid to ask questions. Reputable dealers and breeders are just as concerned with the puppy's welfare as you are.

You can obtain a good list of questions to ask the breeder from the GRCA. This list can also be found by using the words "puppy questions" on the "search GRCA" section of their website. Also included in this list are some questions that the breeders will probably ask you. Do not be offended if a breeder asks questions about your experience with dogs and where you plan to raise your puppy. Take this as a sign of concern. In addition, keep an open line of communication with the breeder so that he or she can help you with any future problems.

Take plenty of time when making your final choice. As previously mentioned, at first all puppies will look cute and very much alike. Watch them carefully, however, and their subtle differences will become more apparent. By watching them play together, you can get a better idea of their individual temperaments. Some may be bolder, others shyer; the puppy's temperament is the best indicator of his adult behavior. Again, do not hesitate to ask for help.

Where and How to Buy a Golden Retriever

Avoid Temptation

You should never be tempted to buy a "cheap" dog. The old adage, "You get what you pay for," is all too true in purchasing a dog. A lower priced dog may mean he was raised strictly for profit by an inexperienced breeder, or that he is in poor health.

Once you have selected the puppy that is best for you, you will have to arrange to take him home. The puppy should be seven weeks old when he moves into his new home. A puppy of this age should adapt very easily to his new environment, yet he should not be old enough to have picked up many bad habits. Studies have shown that during their eighth week, puppies become especially sensitive to environmental changes. If you cannot pick up the puppy during the seventh week, wait until the ninth week. Rather than risk behavioral problems, wait until the puppy is ready for change.

How Much Will It Cost?

Purchase Price

The initial purchase price of a Golden Retriever varies; however, expect to spend at least $500. Puppies from champion-caliber parents may sell for as much as $2000 or more. A younger puppy will usually be less expensive that an older dog, because less time and money will have been invested. The closer an older puppy is to being a show dog, the more expensive he will be. Remember that the extra money you spend initially may save you a great

deal of money on veterinary bills, as well as the heartache that accompanies a poorly reared dog. Licensing fees also vary greatly, so check with your local town hall or animal shelter.

Additional Costs

Food may cost as much as $40 a month, and you must also purchase certain equipment for feeding, grooming, and housing your dog. Veterinary fees must also be considered. A dog requires annual immunizations against all infectious diseases, as well as an annual heartworm test. A puppy may also have to be wormed. If your dog should get sick or injured, he may need additional, costly medical attention.

Finally, you will have to pay a fee to register your dog with the American Kennel Club, as well as annual dues if you join the Golden Retriever Club of America.

You can see that the expenses of owning a Golden Retriever are much greater than the initial purchase price. Therefore, carefully consider these costs before you buy a dog.

HOUSING AND SUPPLIES

Golden owners need to consider the amount of indoor and outdoor space that this medium-large breed requires to keep them in top physical condition and peak mental health.

Indoor Space Requirements

A Golden Retriever, whether a puppy or an adult, needs a reasonably spacious, quiet living area where he can feel comfortable and secure. Inside your home you must provide the dog with a "territory" of his own. This territory will represent your dog's feeding and sleeping areas. In order for your dog to feel protected, these areas should not be moved. Your dog will only feel secure if he has a quiet, reliable place to rest undisturbed. This area should neither isolate the dog nor should it be subject to heavy human traffic.

Good resting areas are most often found in corners where the dog is protected on two sides. These areas should also be draft-free and not in direct sunlight. The dog's sleeping area should also make it easy to confine his movements when you go to bed or when you leave the house.

The Sleeping Area

Your choice of a sleeping box and pad, or a crate with pad, will depend on your method of housebreaking. (See the chapter entitled "Basic and Advanced Training".) I recommend using a crate, as it can also be invaluable for transporting and disciplining your puppy. Dogs are instinctively den animals, and the confined space of a crate will make a puppy feel safer and more comfortable than an open sleeping box.

TIP

Unnecessary Stress

Like his sleeping place, a Golden's feeding place should never be changed. Changes in sleeping and feeding places can cause your pet unnecessary stress. An animal under stress may exhibit behavioral changes, as well as changes in many biological functions, including problems with digestion and excretion. Place your dog's feeding areas in an easily cleaned room such as the kitchen.

Sleeping crate: The crate should be approximately 24 inches (61 cm) high, by 24 inches (61 cm) wide, by 36 inches (91 cm) long. The construction of the crate is important, for it must have strong welds that cannot be broken by a large, active puppy. Fiberglass travel crates are ideal (provided they are of suitable size), as they are constructed extra ruggedly and are easy to clean.

The crate will be your puppy's "house" when you are not around to supervise him. Some crates can also be used to carry your puppy when you go for a drive or to the veterinarian.

Sleeping box: If you decide not to use a crate, purchase a sleeping box. Make sure it is large enough to accommodate a full-grown, spread-out dog. Line the box with shredded newspapers, and then place an old blanket over it. Your dog will find this very comfortable for sleeping. If you decide to build your own box,

use only nonsplintering hardwoods. Because many stains and paints are toxic to puppies, leave the box unfinished.

Keeping Your Golden Outdoors

When you are not home, your Golden will be just as happy (if not happier) outdoors as inside your home. Because a Golden Retriever is family-oriented, do not keep your dog outdoors for very long periods when you are home. If you are outside working, by all means bring your dog with you. During these outdoor periods your Golden will get his daily exercise.

Fences

If you leave your dog outside when you are not home, provide him with a fenced enclosure or run. The run should be at least 6 feet (2 m)

wide, by 15 feet (5 m) long, by 6 feet (2 m) high, and it should be constructed of strong chain-link fence. You can place partially buried boards around the bottom to prevent the dog from digging under the fence. The run can be as large as your yard. However, it must not be smaller than the size stated.

Use a few inches of smooth stone, such as pea gravel, as a base. This will provide drainage when it rains, and it will prevent the dog from becoming muddy. Do not use concrete as a floor, because concrete will retain the smell of urine. The run must also provide your dog with some shade and shelter.

Doghouses

The best form of outdoor shelter is a doghouse. Whether you build your own or buy one, make sure it is raised several inches off the ground to avoid dampness and insects. The doghouse must be properly constructed to protect the dog against wind, rain, and cold, for even a minor draft can lead to serious respira-

tory ailments. The doghouse should be approximately 48 inches (122 cm) long, 36 inches (91 cm) high, and 36 inches (91 cm) wide. If the house is too small, the dog will not be able to stand or sleep comfortably. Also, be sure not to make the house overly large, because during cold weather the dog's body will provide the only form of heat. For this reason, it is also best to insulate the structure.

You can take several precautions in order to keep the house clean. Place a hinged roof on the house for better access. Line the floor with an easy-to-clean material, such as linoleum, above the flooring so that you can spread cedar shavings and cover them with a blanket.

Finally, make sure that (if you live in the northern hemisphere) the opening of the house faces south and is not subject to the cold north winds of winter. You can also hang a piece of canvas or blanket over the opening, making sure it overlaps sufficiently to eliminate drafts. If you live in a climate where winter nights can be very cold, I recommend that you find an indoor place where the dog can sleep—unless you have carefully tested the insulation of the doghouse.

Additional Equipment and Accessories

Your puppy's first day at home can be very busy and hectic. To avoid additional work and confusion, purchase the following items in advance, and keep them available.

✔ The most important pieces of equipment, at least from your dog's point of view, are his food and water dishes. They should be non-breakable and heavy, as well as sturdy enough so that a Golden with a voracious appetite cannot tip them over. Bowls are available in plastic, stainless steel, and ceramic. If you choose a ceramic bowl, make sure it was not fired with a lead-based glaze.

✔ You may have to purchase more than one collar for your dog as he matures. A puppy needs a light collar but not necessarily a strong one. A small puppy requires only a leather or nylon collar, but bear in mind that these tend to deteriorate with time. In addition, your puppy's neck size will increase considerably as he grows, and not all collars adjust sufficiently. Chain collars are strong enough for an adult Golden. I recommend buying your puppy an inexpensive leather or nylon collar and changing to a good chain collar when the dog is nearly full grown. I also recommend purchasing reflecting tags or tape for your dog's collar and leash. These make it easier for a driver to see both dog and master when headlights shine on them, thus making nighttime walks much safer. You should also attach an identity tag with your address and phone number to the dog's collar. This could prove invaluable if your dog ever gets lost.

✔ Leashes come in a wide variety of lengths and materials, and you may want to purchase more than one type. For regular walks, use a leash only a few feet long. This will enable you to quickly bring the dog to your side if you need to. It will also keep the dog from straying too far. If you have sufficient yard space, a 30-foot (9-m) leash with an automatic reel is useful. Remember that Golden puppies will chew—or attempt to chew—anything they can get their teeth on. Therefore, you should not purchase a chain leash for a puppy. Chewing on the chain may damage your puppy's teeth.

✔ Tweezers are helpful in case of external parasites. You will need them to remove ticks.

✔ Golden Retriever owners seldom need muzzles for their dogs. However, you should keep one easily accessible, should the need arise. Some foreign countries require all dogs to wear muzzles, so if you are planning such a trip with your Golden, you may need one. A muzzle is also a good precaution if your dog is hurt and you must bring him to a veterinarian. A dog in severe pain may react unpredictably, so be prepared. When buying a muzzle, be sure you get one that can be adjusted for size. Remember that there is a big difference between the head of a Golden puppy and that of an adult.

Dog Toys

Toys are essential to a dog's well-being. They signify play to a dog, and they let him know that life comprises more than training sessions, eating, and sleeping. Playing with toys gives a dog exercise. In addition, they allow your puppy to develop his survival instincts, as he will attempt to stalk and capture his toys. Giving your puppy toys will also spare your furniture and clothing from teethmarks.

Rawhide bones are excellent for strengthening a Golden's teeth and jaw muscles. A puppy's teeth can quickly chew tough rawhide. Therefore, make sure to replace the bone before it becomes small enough for your puppy to swallow it whole. Avoid toys your puppy can shred and swallow, for they can cause choking or a blockage in the stomach.

Considerations

When choosing toys, make sure they are designed for dogs and are made of nontoxic materials. Some forms of plastic are toxic, and many forms of wood splinter. In addition, be careful with painted items. Some older types of paint contain lead, which if swallowed in excess can be poisonous and even fatal. To be safe, avoid all painted or varnished toys.

TIP

Simple Household Objects

If you are looking for toys around your house, I recommend cardboard boxes and large balls, such as tennis balls. (Golf balls, Ping-Pong balls, and the like should *not* be used, because they can be chewed apart and swallowed.) These simple household objects can entertain a puppy for hours.

A Golden puppy will chew almost anything that will fit into his mouth. He will also tend to seek out anything with your scent, such as your old shoes and clothing. For this reason, keep these items out of your puppy's reach. Also, never give your puppy either your old slippers or toys that resemble valuable objects. To a Golden puppy, there is little difference between a toy slipper and a real one. This is true of anything of value to you: letters, money, keys, baseball gloves, and so on. Keep all valuable items away from your puppy, and you will prevent the development of bad habits.

CARING FOR A GOLDEN RETRIEVER

It is inevitable that your first days home with your new puppy will be rather hectic, but some careful planning can help reduce the worry and stress that both you and your companion will experience.

Before the Puppy Comes Home

Take a few steps now to reduce the confusion when you bring your puppy home. In addition to purchasing necessary equipment and accessories, you should also choose the puppy's food and purchase a supply of it.

When you have bought all the supplies and have placed them in readily accessible locations, begin to "puppy-proof" your home. Remember that a young puppy is very curious, and as he roams through your house he will sniff, paw at, and chew almost everything.

✔ Place all potential hazards out of the puppy's reach.

✔ Remove all poisons, including paints, cleaners, disinfectants, insecticides, and antifreeze. Store them in an area your puppy will have absolutely no access to.

✔ Remove all sharp objects, such as broken glass, nails, and staples. If you have an older home, make sure your dog does not eat paint chips containing lead.

✔ Electrical wires must also be moved out of your puppy's reach. A dog chewing on electrical wires can be injured or killed by the resulting shock.

The First Days Home

Have you ever had to adjust to a new environment, such as a different house, a college dorm, or an apartment? You probably remember feeling loneliness from missing loved ones and friends, and confusion or bewilderment about your new surroundings. In addition, you may have been excited about your new home and your upcoming adventures there. In the same way, the first days home are a very

CHECKLIST

Rules of Puppy Safety

Before you bring your puppy home, review the following seven rules with your family and friends. In addition to preventing injury to the puppy, these rules will help your new pet to feel comfortable and safe in your home.

1. Avoid unnecessary excitement. New owners have a tendency to invite over everyone they know to see their puppy, and young visitors will usually run around, screaming with glee. Let the puppy adjust to his new surroundings before you subject him to numerous strangers.

2. Be sure that everyone in your household knows the proper way to lift and carry the puppy (see page 22). If any visitors express a desire to pick up the puppy, instruct them how to do so.

3. Avoid picking up the puppy too much. Allow him to do his own walking as much as possible, so that he will get needed exercise and added confidence in his own physical abilities.

4. Prohibit rough play. Puppies are fragile creatures and should be handled with care until they grow larger and more mature.

Therefore, you should avoid overhandling, and make sure that children do not prod or poke the puppy, probe into his ears, or subject him to any other rough handling.

5. Do not subject your puppy to unnecessary heights. Avoid placing him on tables, counters, or beds, because a fall could be disastrous. When it is necessary to place the puppy on an elevated surface, as when you are examining or grooming him, someone must be present the entire time to ensure the puppy's safety.

6. Do not give bones or other very hard objects to a young puppy. Until the puppy reaches about six months of age, he has only his milk teeth and cannot chew hard objects such as meat bones.

7. Try never to leave the puppy unsupervised during the first few weeks.

By following these rules, you can keep your puppy safe from harm and increase his confidence in his owner and family. The faster your Golden feels comfortable and safe in his new home, the faster he will begin to act like the loving companion that you envision.

emotional time for your puppy, for he has just entered an unfamiliar world apart from his mother and siblings.

The First Few Hours

The first hours in your home are very important ones for your puppy. At seven weeks of age a Golden puppy is very impressionable.

If a frenzied horde of family and friends greet him at the door, the puppy will believe that hysterical behavior is readily accepted in your home. Introduce your puppy to his new home carefully so he will believe he is entering a safe, calm, rational environment.

When your puppy arrives, he will probably want to urinate or defecate. Instead of entering your house, walk the puppy to a place you have chosen for his elimination area. Give the puppy about ten minutes to relieve himself, and then praise and pet him for doing so. This will help the puppy learn to defecate and urinate outdoors.

In order to help the puppy adjust, let him sniff around your home undisturbed. Then help him learn the location of his food and water dishes. Let your puppy continue to roam about, but feel free to pet him and play with him. When he tires, pick him up and put him in his sleeping box or crate. Within a few days, the puppy should learn where his sleeping area is, and when tired, find his bed on his own.

The next step in training your puppy is the hardest test you will face. Furthermore, it is your first test, and failure here will mean greater problems in the future. Your puppy will

probably whine, whimper, and wail, because he is in an unfamiliar place and because he misses his mother and siblings. It is important, however, that you remain firm. If the puppy sleeps in a crate, do not let him out. If you do, he will wail every time he wants to leave the crate. If you use a sleeping box, you might try to reassure the puppy by speaking softly, but do not take him from the box. Your puppy must learn to deal with loneliness as soon as possible.

Leaving Your Puppy Alone

If you must leave the house during your puppy's first few days, be sure he is not left alone. If no family member is available, ask a neighbor or a close friend to "puppy-sit." An unsupervised, curious Golden Retriever puppy means only one thing: a mess. Your puppy will

TIP

Feeding

1. At first, keep the puppy on the same diet he was receiving from the breeder to minimize digestive system stress. If you want to change the puppy's diet, do it gradually by mixing larger amounts of the new food into the diet while reducing the old food proportionately.

2. Try to feed your puppy on the same schedule as the breeder. If that is inconvenient, gradually shift the feeding times to meet your schedule.

3. From the start, try removing your puppy's food from him (while he is eating) for a few minutes, and then return it to him to continue eating. If you do this regularly, it will reinforce your position as "Master" over your dog, which is critical to successful dog training.

4. Never surprise your dog while he is eating (or sleeping). A surprised dog may react unpredictably, so be sure to explain this rule to your children as well.

investigate his surroundings, using all his instinctive hunting skills. His keen sense of smell will track down various forms of trouble (perhaps the legs of your coffee table or your dining room curtains). Once he spots a target, the puppy will attempt to render it helpless. He will use teeth, paws, and if necessary, all his body weight to accomplish this feat. Hopefully, you will return before the puppy decides to mark off his territory.

Training

Soon after your puppy arrives, you must begin to train him. Training will require time, energy, patience, understanding, and of course, love. From the minute your Golden arrives, begin to teach him his name. Other essential lessons are described in detail in the chapter "Basic and Advanced Training." Remember, the longer you wait to begin training, the harder it will be for your dog to learn.

Lifting and Carrying a Golden Retriever

It is very important for everyone in your family to learn how to lift and carry your puppy. Improper handling can cause pain and even injury.

✔ Place one hand under the puppy's chest and support the rear and hind legs with the other hand. Never pick up the puppy by placing only one hand under his abdomen, and never pick him up by the scruff of the neck. Both of these methods can hurt the puppy.

✔ You should carry an adult Golden only if he is injured or sick. When moving an injured dog, take special precautions. If possible, wait for an experienced person to lift and carry the dog. If you must do this yourself, first place a muzzle on the dog, for a dog in pain may act unpredictably and snap at anyone who tries to help him. Allow the dog to stand, if possible, and slip one arm around the front of the dog, across the front of the shoulder so that his head can rest in the crook of your arm. Slide your other arm under his stomach, in front of his hind legs. Stand up slowly and gently, and avoid jerking. Hold him close to your midsection, and when you have to set

him down, do it gently with his paws toward the floor.

✔ If the dog's weight and size are too great for you, lay him on his side on a blanket or stretcher, and carry him with the help of another person. For further information on treating an injured dog, consult the chapter "Ailments and Illnesses."

Golden Retrievers and Children

One of the greatest pleasures of owning a Golden Retriever is watching him play with children. A mature Golden seems to know instinctively that children are more fragile than adults, and he will be more gentle when playing with youngsters. Younger and more excitable Goldens may have trouble controlling their natural exuberance when playing with children. A Golden puppy plays rambunctiously both with his littermates and with children. Therefore, when a young dog plays with children, he should always be supervised.

A special bond forms between a Golden and children. Golden Retrievers tolerate tremendous pushing, pulling, pinching, and ear and tail tugging from boisterous children. In fact, they seem to enjoy the attention more than they mind the pain. The Golden's coat and skin are extremely tough, for a hunting dog must be able to cope with all types of weather and to run through dense woods and thickets.

However, because the Golden does have vulnerable areas, such as his eyes and nose, teach

your children the proper way to handle their pet. Children should be taught to never disturb a Golden while he is eating or sleeping. Explain that although the dog is a loving pet, he may nip at them if surprised or frightened. Also teach your children how to meet a strange dog. They should not go to the dog, but let him approach them. They should not move suddenly, and they should keep their hands below the dog's head. If the dog sniffs their hands, and is still friendly, it is all right to pet him.

You can help assure an enduring relationship between your children and your Golden by involving them in the responsibilities of dog care. Encourage your children to help feed, groom, and walk your dog.

The Golden and the New Baby

Reports of attacks on infants by family dogs lead many people to get rid of their devoted pets when they have a new baby. This is truly a shame, for Goldens are at their best when they have children—including infants—to love. If you have or are planning to have a baby, take heart. Animal behavior experts who have studied this problem thoroughly have concluded that most dogs will not be aggressive toward a baby. They also believe, however, that dogs that tend to chase and kill small animals, or those that are aggressive toward people in general, should never be left unsupervised with an infant.

You should take several precautions to make sure your Golden will readily accept your new baby.

✔ Train your dog to sit or lie down for long periods of time before the baby is born. As you increase the length of time the dog remains still, accustom him to other activities occurring around him at the same time. Reward your dog if he stays still and does not attempt to follow you.

✔ Once training is complete, simulate the other activities that will occur after the baby arrives. Use a doll to imitate carrying, feeding, changing, and bathing the newborn.

✔ After the birth of the infant, give the dog something the baby used in the hospital so he can sniff and become accustomed to the baby's scent. Upon returning home from the hospital, allow the mother to greet the dog without the baby. Then place the baby in the nursery and deny the dog access by using a screen door or folding gate. In this way the dog can see and hear the infant and get used to its presence before they actually meet.

✔ When you finally introduce dog and baby, one person should control and reward the dog while another person holds the baby. Have the dog sit and then show him to the baby. Keep them together for as long as the dog remains calm. For the next week or two, gradually increase the length of the dog's visit.

✔ Never allow your dog to wander unsupervised in the presence of an infant. However, be sure to include your dog in all the activities that involve your newborn. Do not let the dog feel neglected because of the infant. The more activities in which you allow the dog to participate, the stronger the bond will be between Golden and child.

Goldens and Other Pets

Goldens get along very well with all other pets. Your Golden will rarely show signs of jealousy as long as he receives sufficient attention. If there is a substantial size difference, such as with birds, hamsters, gerbils, and so on, it is best not to allow these animals to play freely with your Golden.

If you own two Goldens, you will rarely have any problems; in fact, the dogs will probably enjoy each other's companionship. You must remember, however, not to give the older dog any less attention than previously. If you show the older dog that you care for him as much as always, you may leave the two to establish their own relationship. You should have very little difficulty getting the two dogs to live together in harmony. In fact, if you show no favoritism to either dog, the older one should adopt and protect the younger one.

The Social Behavior of Dogs

If you plan to own more than one Golden, or if you wish to understand why dogs react as they do to humans and to each other, you must examine the dog's instinctive nature.

Pack Mentality

Canine social behavior is very similar to that of wild wolves. Wolves are pack hunting animals and require companionship. This is also true for Goldens, though humans can thoroughly satisfy their need for company. Because of this need, you can punish a dog by isolating him during training sessions. In addition, as pack animals, dogs develop among themselves a dominant-subordinate relationship. This relationship allows a stable existence between dogs. Thus, if one of your dogs tends to be more dominant than another, do not worry. This occurs naturally and will prevent fights from breaking out between dogs when competitive situations arise relating to food, living space, and human attention. This social ranking is largely determined by size, age, strength, and sex. This social dominance also allows a dog to obey his master, for during training a dog

learns that he is subordinate to the human members of the household.

Both dogs and wolves "mark" their frequently traveled paths or territory by urinating, defecating, and scratching the ground. In addition to such boundary marking, females secrete a scent that signals their being in heat.

Social Considerations for a Female Dog

Precautions Against Pregnancy

If you own a female Golden, you must take special precautions regarding pregnancy. A Golden female normally comes into estrus ("in heat" or "in season") twice a year. Estrus is the period during which the female accepts mating with the male. This period usually lasts three to five days. If you choose not to breed your

female, you can take several measures to prevent pregnancy. As stated earlier, if you plan never to breed or show the female, have her spayed.

The most obvious way to prevent pregnancy, but probably the hardest, is simply to keep your female away from all male dogs. This can be difficult, however, because male dogs will travel a great distance to find a female in heat. During this time, never let your female outside alone, not even in a fenced-in yard. In addition, during this time always walk your female on a leash. The mating urge between the sexes is very great at this time, and the female may be less obedient and not heed your pleas for her to come back.

Many owners who wish to show their females when they are in heat have their veterinarians administer an estrus control medication.

When a female is in heat, a bloody discharge may spot your floors and rugs. If your children ask about the bleeding, assure them that it is entirely natural. To prevent staining of your rugs or furniture, you may want to confine your female to an easy-to-clean room. Sanitary napkins and diapers are available for dogs in heat.

Vacationing with Goldens

Choosing a Kennel

Ideally, you want to have your loving companion accompany you on vacations, but when that is not possible, I recommend having a friend or relative look after him. The best plan is to have a "dog-sitter" stay at your home, or come over when needed. This will allow your dog to stay in a familiar environment. If the person cannot come to your home, perhaps the person can keep your Golden in his/her house while you are away.

If you cannot find a trustworthy person, you will need to look into other alternatives. You can try contacting the breeder from whom you got your dog to see if he/she would be willing to look after your dog while you are away. If this is

not possible, you may wish to place the dog in a boarding kennel. If you plan to do this, be sure to carefully inspect the kennel before leaving your dog there. Golden Retrievers are people oriented, and many kennels cannot provide the social contact they need. If the kennel can provide the human contact and if the facilities are clean and well managed, a mature Golden should have little problem adjusting. You should never leave a puppy younger than six months old at a boarding kennel if you can avoid it.

Traveling with Your Golden

Of course, you can also take your dog with you. Although this may require some planning and hard work, it can be done.

By air: If you plan to travel by air anywhere in the United States or abroad, you'll be glad to know that many airlines accept dogs. Those airlines will supply a large crate and will transport your dog in the pressurized cabins of the luggage compartment. Check the cost and any rules concerning pet transport ahead of time.

By rail: All major railroads transport dogs throughout the United States. Most will transport large dogs only if they travel in a shipping crate in the baggage car. Check with the railroad to see whether or not they supply the crate.

By car: When traveling by car, your dog may ride either in his crate or in the back seat. Open the window enough to give him some fresh air, but do not expose him to a draft. Drafts can cause eye, ear, and throat problems. Make rest stops at least every two hours and allow your dog to walk and relieve himself. Keep him on a leash so that he will not run away. The inside of a car can get very hot, so allow your dog to drink regularly. Keep a bottle of water on the floor so it remains cool.

Many young dogs become carsick if they are not used to traveling. To prevent this, obtain tablets for motion sickness from your veterinarian.

Traveling Abroad

If you are traveling abroad, obtain a copy of the country's laws pertaining to dogs. Check the website, or e-mail the consulate of the country you plan to visit, and request a copy. Most countries have minimal requirements concerning dogs; however, some do have special quarantine regulations. You must also be aware of regulations concerning vaccinations, and you will need a valid health certificate from a licensed veterinarian. In addition, you will need a current certificate of vaccination against rabies (not more than six months old). If you need a veterinarian while traveling abroad, you can get a list from the American consulate or embassy in the country you are visiting.

Grooming your Golden Retriever is a simple task that should take no more than about a half hour. You should groom the dog at least once every two weeks.

Equipment

In order to keep your Golden in top condition you will need the following equipment: pin brush, slicker brush, comb, scissors or electric clipper, nail clippers, styptic powder, toothbrush, and canine toothpaste (available from your veterinarian).

Professional groomers may use a wider variety of equipment, such as wide and narrow tooth combs, bristle brushes, or a stripping knife. However, for the purpose of routine grooming, these extra tools may not be needed.

Coat Care

Start by giving your dog a thorough brushing. Use a slicker brush on the major portions of the body. Gently untangle any matted hair or knots with the slicker brush, being careful not to pull out the hair or cause the dog pain by brushing too vigorously. Then brush the coat again using a pin brush. You should feel no tangles as you brush through the coat. Also use the pin brush for the feathering on the legs, chest, and tail. After brushing, comb the entire coat to remove any loose hairs that the brushing may have missed.

While brushing, look for signs of external parasites, such as fleas and ticks. If you see any, treat the dog immediately. These parasites may

be harder to eliminate if you leave them to multiply. If you note any unusual skin conditions, contact your veterinarian for advice.

Some Goldens grow a great deal of soft hair on or around their ears, which may be trimmed to improve their appearance. In addition, you can trim any long or straggly hair growing around the edge of the ears. You should also trim the hair between the pads of your dog's feet. Cut this hair as short as possible. This will reduce the chance of infection in damp weather and will also improve the dog's traction. Trim the dog's feathering if it becomes excessively long.

Bathing

The Golden Retriever is a double-coated breed. Excessive bathing will promote the shedding of the undercoat, so bathe your dog only when necessary. If the dog's underside or legs are dirty, wash them with a wet, soapy cloth.

When a bath is necessary, purchase a high-quality dog shampoo. After shampooing, be sure to rinse out the shampoo thoroughly. Soap that is not rinsed out may irritate your dog's skin. If you wish, use a cream rinse to give the coat more body and make the

Check on the condition of your Golden's teeth and gums at least once a week.

hair easier to comb. Then towel the dog dry. Rub the dog briskly with a large towel to remove most of the water. Then brush and comb his coat. Keep the dog indoors and away from drafts while he is drying.

Trimming the Nails

If your dog is active and gets plenty of exercise, you will not need to trim his nails regularly. However, nails can grow back quickly on a "house dog," which may require frequent trimming. Before you trim your dog's nails, be sure you learn how to use a pair of clippers. Improper use of nail clippers can cause your dog a great deal of pain. An experienced dog groomer or a veterinarian can show you how to use them. The center of a dog's nail (called the "quick") contains a blood vessel and nerve endings. You can see these when you examine the dog's claws. If you cut the quick, your dog will suffer much pain.

The quick grows out as your dog's nail lengthens. If you wait too long between pedicures, you may have to cut the quick in order to clip the nail back to a comfortable length. Always clip the nail as close to the quick as possible, and be sure to hold the dog's paws firmly but gently. If you accidentally cut the nail too short, it will bleed. Stop the bleeding by using styptic powder.

Tooth Care

Proper tooth care begins with feeding your Golden plenty of hard foods, such as dog biscuits and rawhide bones, to help prevent the buildup of tartar. Excessive tartar can lead to deterioration of the gums and tooth loss. Brush your dog's teeth once a week with a toothbrush, using a special canine toothpaste. Before brushing, check the dog's teeth and gums for signs of infection or tartar buildup. Excessive

When examining your Golden's ears, lift the flaps so you have an unobstructed view, and be very careful when probing into the inner ear.

tartar buildup will have to be scraped off by your veterinarian.

Ear and Eye Care

As part of your daily grooming routine, be sure to check that your dog's ears are free of wax and dirt, and his eyes are clear and free of discharge. You can clean around your dog's eyes using a moistened cotton ball to remove any dirt. Use a fresh cotton ball for each eye. If you notice any discharge or inflammation, consult your veterinarian for advice. To clean your Golden's ear, hold it open with one hand and gently clean the inside of the flap with a small piece of moistened cotton. Again, use a fresh piece for each ear. Be careful not to probe too deeply into the ear canal.

Caution: Before cleaning your dog's eyes and ears for the first time, I recommend that you consult with your veterinarian for the proper way to clean and care for them. An inexperienced owner can cause serious harm to a dog by probing around his ears and eyes. Once you have learned the proper procedures, you will be able to care for these sensitive organs with confidence.

WHAT DO I FEED MY DOG?

The nutritional requirements of dogs have probably not changed very much from the time they were first domesticated. Our understanding of those needs, however, has increased greatly in recent years.

The National Research Council (NRC), a division of the National Academy of Sciences, has interpreted vast quantities of data and published a study entitled "The Nutritional Requirements of Dogs." This study establishes the minimum amount of every nutrient—protein, fat, carbohydrates, vitamins, minerals, and trace elements—needed to maintain the health of the average middle-aged and older dogs, as well as growing puppies.

The NRC study serves as a guideline for all companies that manufacture commercial dog food in the United States to help them formulate their products. In fact, for a dog food to be certified as "complete and balanced" in the Unites States, it must meet or exceed all of the nutritional requirements established by the NRC. In addition, it must also pass actual feeding tests established by the Association of American Feed Control Officials (AAFCO).

While their ancestors (wolves) are scientifically classified as carnivores, modern domestic dogs have evolved to effectively utilize a wide variety of foods to meet their nutritional needs, and are therefore considered omnivores. This allows modern commercial dog food manufacturers to use a wide variety of ingredients to achieve the mandated nutritional profiles. Unfortunately, for the consumer, it can make it very hard to determine which dog food is best for your Golden Retriever. To help decide, seek the advice of your breeder and veterinarian. Breeders will know what food works best for their Goldens, while veterinarians have a working knowledge of dog foods based on the experiences of other clients. A veterinarian will also be able to recommend a special diet should your Golden's health dictate the need for one.

I strongly urge all dog owners to use a high-quality commercial dog food rather than preparing their pet's food from scratch. When preparing meals at home, it can be difficult to determine if you are giving your loving com-

Nutrient Reference Chart

Nutrient (Sources)	Nutritional Value and Symptoms of Deficiencies
Protein (Meat; Eggs; Fish; Milk; Soybean Meal; Brewer's Yeast; Wheat Germ)	Provides amino acids for essential growth, development, maintenance of strong bones and muscles. Promotes production of antibodies, enzymes, and hormones. Deficiencies include poor growth, weight loss, loss of appetite, and poor hair and coat.
Fat (Meat; Vegetable Oils)	Source of energy and heat. Supplies essential fatty acids and fat-soluble vitamins. Needed to keep skin and coat in top condition. Deficiencies include dry and coarse coat and skin lesions.
Carbohydrates (Sugars; Starches)	Help regulate energy balance. Fiber and roughage help regulate digestive system and help prevent diarrhea/constipation.
Vitamins (Brewer's Yeast; Vegetables; Fruits; Cod Liver Oil; Wheat Germ Oil)	Important in preventing numerous illnesses and diseases. Help in regulating many bodily functions, including growth and fertility.
Minerals/Trace Elements (Bones; Meat; Grains; Fruit; Vegetables)	Help prevent many ailments and diseases. Regulate many bodily functions, including bone formation. Helps regulate water balance.

panion too much or too little of an essential nutrient. It is also significantly more expensive and much more time-consuming. This is quality time you can use playing and exercising with your beloved pet. However, if you feel that, as an act of love, you want to prepare your dog's food from scratch, I strongly advise you to read as many books as you can on animal nutrition and seek the advice of your veterinarian.

What Is High-Quality Dog Food?

Like human food recipes, the ingredients used to make commercial dog foods have varying degrees of nutritional value. While most "complete diets" are supplemented with a sufficient quantity of vitamins and minerals, the ingredients used in a high-quality dog food should be easily digestible and free of chemical additives which, over the long term, can have harmful effects on your pet.

When looking for a high-quality diet, check the label to make sure the pet food was tested using AAFCO procedures, and is complete and balanced. This statement can be found at the end of the nutritional information panel on the dog food label.

Check the list of ingredients. By law, the label must contain a list of ingredients, with the most abundant ingredient (by percent weight) listed first, and the remaining ingredients listed

in the order of decreasing weight. The primary ingredients listed in a high-quality dog food should be easily recognizable, such as chicken, beef, lamb, brown rice, carrots, and peas. Ingredients such as cornmeal, wheat, soy, and white rice are carbohydrate fillers that are not easy to digest and provide little nutritional value. Be extra cautious with wheat- and soy-based products as they are both allergens. Look for foods that use meat meals rather than animal "by-products." Meat meal is actually meat with the water removed, whereas "by-products" contain the indigestible parts of animals including feet, feathers, hooves, and hair. Finally, avoid foods that contain chemical antioxidants such as BHA and BHT. High-quality dog food will use Vitamin C or Vitamin E instead to prevent fats from turning rancid.

Feeding Table Scraps

Many people feel that they are obliged as loving pet owners to feed their precious pooches leftovers. Be warned that this practice has great potential for teaching your Golden really bad habits such as begging. Feeding the wrong table scraps to your Golden can lead to obesity, which in turn can lead to health issues later on. I have also seen instances where this practice can lead to a dog refusing to eat his regular diet, which can also result in problems related to malnutrition.

How Many Meals Do I Feed My Golden?

Relative to their body weight, dogs can eat larger quantities of food than humans at a sin-

and must constantly replenish whatever they lose. This means that you must make sure your dog has an adequate supply of water at all times. A Golden's water intake will depend on several factors, including air temperature, the type of food he eats, the amount of exercise he gets, and his temperament. Be sure to avoid giving your dog very cold water, especially after strenuous exercise or if he is showing signs of heatstroke. Cooling the dog's body down too fast can be counterproductive and lead to other severe illnesses.

Does My Golden Need Nutritional Supplements?

Nutitional Supplements for dogs is currently a very controversial topic of discussion. While there is plenty of information available, it is often difficult to separate the information that comes from the manufacturers of nutritional supplements from that of independent researchers.

Naturally, the manufacturers of these items are interested in selling their products, but as with humans, getting too much of some nutrients (such as vitamin D) can be toxic and have dangerous side effects. The amount of nutrients your Golden needs will depend on several factors including diet, age, activity level, medical conditions, and environmental stresses. This means that not all dogs need nutritional supplements, but some may have very specific needs. Before you give your dog any supplement, particularly vitamins or minerals, you should consult your veterinarian. He or she will review with you the critical factors affecting your dog's nutritional requirements before giving you advice.

gle meal, so they do not need to be fed as frequently. Adults can be fed one or two times a day, while puppies need to be fed more often. A puppy between one and three months old needs to be fed at least four times a day. Because dogs react well to routines, you should create a schedule that you can commit to and stick with on a regular basis. A good time to feed your dog is during the family meals, so he is occupied while the rest of the family is at the dinner table.

The Importance of Water

Of all the components of a dog's diet, there is none more important than water. Water is vital to every living cell and comprises nearly 60 percent of your dog's body weight. Unlike some animals, dogs cannot store much water

Special Considerations for Feeding Your Golden

While the NRC provides the minimum nutritional requirements for puppies as well as adult and older dogs, several other factors affect the type and quantity of food an individual dog needs. Growing puppies require about twice the amount of calories per pound of body weight as a middle-aged adult, while older dogs require about 20 percent less than an average adult.

As a result, puppies need special diets that are higher in proteins and fats to support their growth and metabolic needs, while older dogs, with their slower metabolism, can become overweight if their diet is not changed. Exercise, work performed, and environment will also influence the quantity of food your Golden needs. Goldens that get a lot of exercise, are used for hunting, or participate in numerous field and obedience trials will usually require

a diet that is higher in calories. The same is true for dogs that spend a lot of time outdoors in the cold weather.

The best indicators that your companion is getting the proper amount of nutrition are his body weight and coat condition. Your dog is at an ideal weight if you can feel his ribs and can easily discern the waist from the ribs when looking from above. You should also be able to feel the abdomen tucked up. If you have an underweight Golden, you will easily see his ribs, vertebrae, and pelvic bones, and you will not feel any fat on the bones. Severely malnourished dogs lose muscle mass, and puppies will have stunted growth. When a Golden is overweight, you cannot feel the ribs and you may see fat bulges over the dog's back. In addition, the waist will not be discernible from the ribs and the abdomen will drop. A dry coat and flaky skin may signify a fat, fatty acid, or vitamin deficiency. This condition is often

accompanied by scratching and is often misdiagnosed by pet owners as external parasites or other skin ailments. The proper diet should produce a soft and shiny coat that is rich in color.

A Final Note on Feeding a Dog

You should know that dogs do not require a wide variety of foods and will not tire from eating the same thing every day. If you feed your Golden a high-quality, well-balanced diet, he can thrive on that food for most of his life. If your dog is not eating properly, it may be an indicator of a physical or emotional problem. If your Golden doesn't follow his normal diet for a day or two, there may not be any reason to worry and the dog's appetite may return on its own. But if your dog refuses to eat for more than two days, it may be a sign of a serious problem, and the dog should be taken to the veterinarian for an examination.

AILMENTS AND ILLNESSES

Dogs, like humans, are subject to a wide variety of illnesses. While the Golden Retriever is no exception, you will be glad to know that there are several things you can do to prevent many of the ailments described in this chapter.

Proper nutrition, good hygiene, and an adequate exercise program are essential in keeping your Golden healthy. These basic requirements combined with scheduled visits to the veterinarian can help your Golden live a long and healthy life. You must never underestimate the importance of keeping scheduled appointments with your veterinarian. Early detection is the key to preventing many problems from getting out of hand, and it sometimes takes a trained medical eye to detect early symptoms.

Choosing a Veterinarian

The worst time to look for a veterinarian is when you really need one, so make sure you have chosen your veterinarian before you bring your new Golden home. When looking for a veterinarian, keep in mind that you are looking for more than a medical expert. You are looking for someone to meet the needs of both you and your pet—someone with "people" as well as "animal" skills.

Like your doctor, veterinarians often work with a staff of professionals (technicians, administrators, and aids), so you will likely want to evaluate the competence and caring of the entire team. Location, fees, facility cleanliness, and suitability are also very important factors that you will need to evaluate. Weigh all of the issues that are important to you, but remember you will probably be happier if you drive a few extra miles or pay a few extra dollars to get the care you want for your companion.

The best way to find a good veterinarian is to ask people who have the same approach to pet care as you. Look for recommendations from friends, breeders, animal shelters, dog trainers, groomers, and/or pet sitters. Once you have narrowed your search, schedule a visit to meet the staff, tour the facility, and learn about the veterinary philosophy on treatment.

Once you feel you have completed your research, it is time to make your decision. Only you can determine what factors are the most

important, but under no circumstances should this decision ever be made based on cost alone.

What Are Symptoms?

Simply put, symptoms are indicators of diseases or disorders; and because dogs cannot talk, symptoms provide the only signs your pet is not feeling well. Although understanding the symptoms, or combinations of symptoms, associated with certain ailments may help you narrow down the possibilities, the trained eye of a veterinarian is usually required to determine the exact cause of your Golden's illnesses or ailments.

Symptoms to Watch For

There are several symptoms of which every dog owner should be aware. If you notice any one, or combination of them, you should call your veterinarian. Be alert for:
- ✔ exhaustion
- ✔ loss of appetite or thirst
- ✔ excessive appetite or thirst
- ✔ unusual sneezing or wheezing
- ✔ excessive coughing
- ✔ runny nose
- ✔ discharge from the eyes or ears
- ✔ poor coat condition
- ✔ foul breath
- ✔ blood in the stool
- ✔ slight paralysis
- ✔ limping, trembling, or shaking
- ✔ swelling or lumps on the body
- ✔ sudden weight loss
- ✔ cloudy or orange colored urine
- ✔ inability to urinate
- ✔ uncontrolled urination
- ✔ moaning or whimpering
- ✔ unusual slobbering or salivation
- ✔ vomiting
- ✔ diarrhea

The last two on the list, vomiting and diarrhea, are probably the most common of all canine symptoms; however, they do not always indicate the presence of a serious ailment. For example, young dogs sometimes wolf down their food with such speed that their natural defense mechanisms send it right back up again. It is also common to see a dog eat grass and subsequently vomit in a voluntary attempt to purge the digestive tract. While this behavior is completely natural, it may not necessarily be an indicator that a larger problem exists. Persistent vomiting, however, can indicate a very serious ailment and should be reported to your veterinarian immediately. It can be caused by several digestive disorders and diseases and is often accompanied by irregular bowel movements, including diarrhea.

Likewise, the occasional soft stool is usually nothing to worry about. During the warmer summer months, dogs tend to drink more water and, as a result, their stools may become loose or they may even get diarrhea. Short-term acute diarrhea can also be caused by minor stomach upsets. Acute diarrhea starts suddenly and lasts for a few days to a week. Most cases of acute diarrhea can be handled at home by changing your dog's diet. Try using a diet that is half boiled rice and half cooked chicken. Do not restrict your Golden's water intake when he has diarrhea, and be sure to keep offering him a clean, fresh supply.

Chronic diarrhea, continuous or frequent watery bowel movements, where your dog is acting sick during the worst bouts, can indicate a serious problem. Long-standing diarrhea can become a severely debilitating disorder. It can cause your dog's body to lose valuable nutrients, impair immune system functions, and lose the ability to properly detoxify. This can lead to the development of secondary disorders that will become even harder to treat. Whenever you see the signs of chronic diarrhea, bring it to the immediate attention of your veterinarian.

Immunization: The Pros and Cons

Before the discovery of vaccines, several infectious diseases ran rampant through the canine population, leading to a large number of deaths. Thankfully, advances in modern medical science led to the development of vaccines that can protect dogs against the bacteria and viruses that cause most major infectious diseases. While all vaccines are extremely effective, not all are needed by every dog, and not all offer permanent protection.

For years the standard practice was to give dogs scheduled booster shots, and in some cases, the frequency in which they were given was determined by local law. This "better safe than sorry" practice is presently the topic of heavy debate. Homeopaths have long argued against frequent vaccination, claiming that vaccines are not as benign as first believed, and dogs that are vaccinated excessively or needlessly are subject to more diseases and disorders than dogs that are not. In reaction to this argument, many veterinary schools have begun researching the effects of vaccines to determine if the effect they have on the long-term health of the dog outweighs the benefits gained from the presently recommended vaccination protocol.

Another approach being used to determine the need to re-vaccinate is called "titer" (titre) testing. This test is used to determine the levels of specific disease-fighting antibodies the dog has in his bloodstream. If the titer test reveals sufficient levels of a specific disease-fighting antibody, it is a good indicator that the dog has immunity against the disease and re-vaccination is not needed. Unfortunately, a low or absent titer does not always indicate that the dog does not have immunity.

A dog's immune system has a "memory" and will not expend energy developing unnecessary antibodies if it has the ability to produce more within a day or two of exposure to an infectious organism. While titer testing will tell if a dog has a level of antibody to give him a reasonable chance to fight a disease, it can give false negatives that could lead to unnecessary booster vaccinations.

So where does this leave the average dog owner? My recommendation is to treat vaccine administration as a medical procedure, and as such, the benefits as well as risks need to be considered when making the decision to use them. Talk to your veterinarian about your concerns. In return, listen to the reasoning he uses, which comes from practical experience, in determining the frequency recommended for vaccination. If you believe that your veterinarian has your pet's best interest in mind, the choice is usually very easy. Keep in mind, however, that sometimes the frequency of vaccination, particularly for rabies, may be required by local law.

Infectious Diseases and Vaccines

Vaccines are now divided into two classes in the United States. "Core" vaccines are those that the American Veterinary Medical Association (AVMA) recommends should be given to every dog, and "non-core" vaccines that are limited to certain dogs, depending on their species and environment. The choice to use non-core vaccines depends on a number of variables, including age, breed, the health status of the dog, the potential of exposure, the type of vaccine, and how common the disease is to the geographical area where the dog lives. So, dogs that are not boarded probably do not need all the vaccinations against "kennel cough," and the Lyme disease vaccine should be administered only if you live in an area where it is prevalent. It is important to note that some core and non-core vaccines are given by veterinarians in what are called "combination vaccines." These are single injections that will deliver the vaccines for as many as five different contagious diseases. Determining what "combination" and non-core vaccines as well as the type and frequency of booster immunizations your dog receives is a decision that you will have to make with the advice of your veterinarian.

The four core vaccines immunize your Golden against canine distemper, canine hepatitis, parvovirus, and rabies. Recently, however, a report from the AVMA recommends adding canine adenovirus-2 (presently classified as non-core) to the core vaccines. Non-core vaccines also exist for bordetellosis, parainfluenza, leptospirosis, coronavirus, and Lyme disease. Chances are that your breeder will have your puppy up-to-date on his immunizations when you get him. As it takes three to four weeks for the first set of immunizations to become completely effective, it would be wise to keep your new puppy away from all non-immunized animals until the vaccines can take full effect.

Of Worms and Worming

Worms are by far the most common internal parasite found in dogs. There are four major types of worms that live in the digestive tract of the infected animal—roundworms, hookworms, whipworms, and tapeworms—and one major type that attacks the heart muscle—heartworms. The eggs of the digestive tract worms, and sometimes adult worms themselves, can be found in the dog's stool. The eggs are microscopic, so if you suspect your dog has worms you will have to take a stool sample to the veterinarian so the proper medication can be given.

Roundworms

Roundworms are parasites that are commonly found in young dogs. They are white, cylindrical in shape, and can grow up to 4 inches (10 cm) long. During their life cycle, roundworm larvae migrate through various organs in the dog's body and will finish their migration in the intestinal tract, where they become adults and lay their eggs, which are then passed out with the stool. The larvae will also migrate to the womb of pregnant females, where they can infest the unborn puppies. If the eggs are ingested by another animal, they will grow into adults in their new host and thus continue the cycle. While roundworms are rarely harmful to an adult dog, they can be fatal to a puppy.

Symptoms of roundworm include diarrhea, cramps, irregular appetite, weakness, poor coat condition, bloated belly, and in severe cases, paralysis. They can be treated with an oral de-worming medication. All fecal matter expelled during the treatment phase needs to be picked up and disposed of to keep the dog from ingesting more eggs. There are heartworm medications on the market that are also effective in controlling not only roundworms, but hookworms, whipworms, and tapeworms as well.

Roundworms pose a pubic health hazard, as the larvae can penetrate human skin and affect various organs in the body. Avoid being barefoot before and during treatment, and wash thoroughly after cleaning up after your Golden.

Hookworms

Hookworms are also most commonly seen in younger dogs, live in the intestines, and pass their eggs out in the host's stool. Sometimes adult worms are seen in the feces. They are light in color and resemble strings of spaghetti. Dogs become infected by eating the eggs, or by penetration of the footpads or skin by the larvae. Hookworms can also be transmitted through a nursing mother's milk, or passed from a mother to her unborn puppies. Hookworm infestations can cause fatal anemia in young, weak, or malnourished dogs.

Symptoms include weight loss, diarrhea, and bloody stools. Treatment also includes treating anemia if it accompanies the infestation. Since hookworms are also public health threats, follow the same precautions as you would for roundworms regarding cleanup, personal sanitization, and apparel.

Whipworms

Whipworms are normally seen in dogs that are three months of age or older, as the eggs will not be seen in the stool until three months after the infection. The adult worms live in the large intestine and the eggs are passed through the stool. Diagnosis can sometimes be difficult because, unlike all of the other digestive tract worms, whipworms are not prolific egg layers. Infection occurs when a dog eats contaminated fecal matter.

Symptoms of whipworm infestations include weight loss and diarrhea that is sometimes tinted with blood. These worms are usually not seen in the stool. Treatment consists of using an oral dewormer with follow-up doses.

Tapeworms

Adult tapeworms live in the intestines of dogs and are transmitted by eating fleas that have in turn ingested tapeworm eggs. Some forms of tapeworms can also be carried by small mammals and, if ingested, can grow in the new host. The head of the worm has a series of hooks that it uses to attach itself tenaciously to a dog's small intestine. The body of a tapeworm grows in a long, segmented chain, with the tail section containing many eggs. On occasion the worm will release the egg–containing section that is then passed out in the stool. These sections look like grains of rice and often stick to the hairs of the dog's anus.

The symptoms of tapeworm infestations take a long time to develop and include poor coat condition, irritability, diarrhea, and lethargy. Treatment is with an oral or injectable dewormer. Control of infestations can be achieved by preventing exposure of the dog to fleas. While people can become infected from certain species of tapeworms that are found in dogs, these instances are very rare.

Heartworm

While once found only along the southeastern seacoast, heartworm can now be found throughout the United States and is transmitted through mosquito bites. There are presently more than 60 species of mosquitoes known to transmit this illness. Heartworms spend their adult life attached to both the right side of a dog's heart and the large blood vessels that attach the heart to the lungs. They can also be found in other species of animals but are rarely seen in humans.

Severely infected dogs can host several hundred adult heartworms that can live for five to seven years. This puts a very great strain on an infected dog's heart, which becomes enlarged, has to work harder, ages rapidly, and eventually weakens. Adult worms can obstruct the heart chambers and blood vessels between the heart and lungs. If a worm dies it can block the flow of blood to smaller vessels, thus causing any number of circulation-related problems. Symptoms include coughing, decreased appetite, weight loss, and lethargy. In rare situations where infestations are very severe, the dog may die of sudden heart failure.

The best way to deal with heartworms is to use preventive medications, but it is important to understand that these do not kill the adult worms. In addition, if preventives are used when adult heartworms are present, other severe problems can result. Therefore, it is very important to have your dog tested by your veterinarian for the presence of heartworms before any medications are started. If the fully grown worms are present, they need to be treated with an adulticide or through surgical procedures.

There are a number of heartworm preventives available, and some will also help control other parasites. The two most popular are ivermectin and milbemycin. It is suggested that preventive medications be used year-round, even in areas where mosquitoes occur seasonally. If given continuously, the preventive medication will stop the worms from developing into adults. The choice of medications should be discussed with your veterinarian so you can learn the pros and cons of each.

External Parasites

During the course of practically every dog's life, he will experience some form of discomfort that will be caused by external parasites, such as fleas, ticks, or mites. These parasites can be

extremely irritating to pets (as well as their owners), and cause serious skin problems. In addition,
they can be the carriers of many diseases.

Fleas

The most common of canine parasites, fleas
cause more pain and suffering than any other
ailment. Fleas flourish when the weather turns
warm and humid, so depending on the climate
in which you live, fleas may be a seasonal or
year-round problem. They differ from other
parasites in that their strong hind legs enable
them to jump long distances from one dog (or
other warm-blooded host) to another. Adult
fleas are dark brown and about the size of a
sesame seed. They are highly mobile and, once
they crawl under a dog's thick coat, they can
move rapidly over his skin.

You may not know when your pet has a
small infestation, but it is possible for ten adult
fleas to produce well over 250,000 offspring in

a month, so if left untreated it will be only a
matter of time before your Golden begins to
show obvious signs of discomfort. Symptoms of
flea infestation range from mild redness of skin
to severe scratching that can lead to open
sores and skin infections. Another sign of flea
infestation is the presence of small black flea
"droppings"—about the size of fine ground
black pepper—that the parasite leaves on your
pet's coat. The excrement is dried blood meal,
so if you put some of the powder on a damp
white tissue it will turn a rusty red-brown color
as it dissolves. You may also see adult fleas
along with the excrement if you use a flea
comb on the infested dog.

Fleas feed by biting their host and sucking
its blood, so a Golden with heavy flea infestations can become anemic. Some dogs are allergic to flea saliva, which results in even more
irritation and scratching. Where infestations
are very heavy, fleas have been known to bite
humans. With modern medicines, prevention
of flea infestations is now much easier and
safer than it was in the past. There are several
topical flea adulticides on the market today,
including imidacloprid and fipronil, which are
very effective preventives and last up to 30
days per dose. They do not require the flea to
ingest blood and can kill the flea before it bites
or lays eggs.

Ticks

These dangerous bloodsucking parasites can
be found in just about every country in the
world. They are of particular concern because
some of them carry and transmit disease.

Tick populations and the diseases associated
with them vary demographically. The most
common tick found in the United States is the

"brown dog tick," which is large enough to be seen with the human eye. While not all brown ticks are dangerous, it has been implicated as a carrier of Rocky Mountain spotted fever and Babesiosis. These two diseases have similar symptoms, including fever, anorexia, depression, lethargy, and a rapid pulse rate. Another disease carrier is the deer tick, which is much smaller and barely perceptible to the human eye. It is this diminutive tick that is responsible for the spread of Lyme disease.

Dogs that frequent grassy and wooded areas populated by wild mammals have the greatest risk of exposure to ticks. Both the nymph and adult stages feed on animals. Unfed ticks resemble small crawling bugs, but once they attach themselves and begin to feed on their host, they begin to swell with blood until they look like a dried raisin. As they continue to gorge, they swell like a miniature balloon. Ticks are most often found around a dog's neck, in the ears, in the folds between the legs and body, and between the toes. Tick bites can cause skin irritation, and heavy infestations can cause anemia. If you take your Golden to tick-prone areas for fun or exercise, be sure to examine him for ticks immediately upon returning home and remove them at once. Prompt removal of ticks is very important, because it lessens the chance of disease transmission. Pets at risk for ticks can be treated using preventive flea adulticides. Your veterinarian can recommend the product best suited to your needs.

Lice

Like most external parasites, lice are bloodsuckers, and their bite causes irritation. They will spend their entire lives among the hair of their hosts. When they lay their eggs (called

nits), they become firmly attached to the victim's hair. If your dog is infested, you can see the egg clusters attached to the hairs. Lice can be very dangerous, so bring your dog to the veterinarian if you spot eggs. Lice can be readily treated with insecticidal products.

Of Mites and Mange

Mites are very small parasites that do their damage by burrowing into a dog's skin, causing intense itching. Mites are no bigger than a pinhead and require a microscope for proper indentification. When they burrow into the skin in large numbers, they can cause a serious skin disease called mange. While mange can occur in healthy dogs, a clean, sanitary environment is the best deterrent. This condition is more typically found in dogs that frequent unsanitary places and suffer from improper nutrition. There are three principle forms of mites that infest dogs: ear mites, sarcoptic mange mites, and demodectic mange mites.

Ear mites are common in young dogs and generally confine themselves to the ear and surrounding areas. Ear mites can cause an intense irritation of the ear canal, which can cause the infested dog to excessively shake his head or scratch his ears, sometimes to the point where bleeding sores are created. A black or brown ear discharge is another sign of ear mite infestation. This ailment can be treated by cleaning the ear and applying topical medications to the affected area.

Sarcoptic mange mites cause sarcoptic mange (scabies). They are highly contagious and are transmitted through close contact, bedding, or grooming tools. These mites burrow into the skin, causing severe itching, hair loss, skin rashes, and crusting/scabbing of the affected areas. Infections can develop as a secondary result. People who come into close contact with an affected dog can develop skin rashes. Treatment of this ailment requires medication to kill the mites and additional treatments to relieve the itching and cure any infections. Cleaning and sanitizing the affected dog's environment is also necessary.

Demodectic mange mites are microscopic and cause demodectic mange. This is not as contagious, but it can be passed from a mother to her puppies. Unlike the other forms of mange, demodectic mange may indicate an underlying medical condition, so the victim's health must be carefully monitored, and treatment options will need to be discussed with your veterinarian. A veterinarian can identify the type of mange in question by taking a skin sample and examining it under a microscope. Once the type of mange has been identified, the proper treatment can begin.

Other Skin Disorders

Additional skin disorders include allergies, eczema, and ringworm. Allergic symptoms may be similar to those of other skin ailments: inflammation, itching, pimples, flaking or scaling, and sometimes skin loss. Treatment usually takes time, because your veterinarian must locate the specific cause.

Eczema is a general name for skin irritations that cannot be clearly identified. Eczema occurs in either wet or dry patches, and it may have many causes, including dietary deficiencies of vitamin A and fat, exposure to dampness or excessive heat, hormone imbalance, and parasites.

Ringworm is not a worm but a fungus that usually attacks the outer layer of a dog's skin. It resembles mange in many respects, causing inflammation, itching, and hair loss that uncovers a scabby area. Ringworm may be carried from an infected dog to a human or vice versa, so prompt veterinary treatment is essential.

Digestive Disorders

Constipation

Constipation occurs when solid waste products that cannot be easily passed build up in the dog's

digestive tract. Generally, this can be relieved by changing the dog's diet and by including a mild laxative as recommended by your veterinarian.

Obstipation, which may be confused with constipation, is caused by eating an indigestible object, such as a small toy or a stone. If you suspect this, call your veterinarian immediately. Do not give your dog a laxative if you suspect a foreign substance. This can be alleviated only by surgically removing the object.

Gastric Dilation and Volvulus (GDV)

GDV can happen very rapidly and often proves to be fatal. It occurs when a dog's stomach fills with gas and/or fluids, swells, and sometimes may even twist on its own axis. If this happens, a dog may go into shock. If bloating occurs, immediate veterinary care (surgery) is required if the dog's life is to be saved.

GDV often occurs after the following scenario; the dog eats a large meal, drinks a lot of water, and is then exercised within two or three hours of eating. The symptoms of GDV are restlessness, and the dog's belly will appear swollen and firm.

Although diet and management changes will not protect every dog, you can reduce the risk by following these suggestions:

1. Feed your dog two or three smaller meals a day rather than one large meal (or you can make dry food available throughout the day, allowing the dog to eat at will).

2. Restrict water intake after feedings; or if dry food is offered two or three times a day, add water to it first and let the food absorb it. This way, the dog's stomach fills faster and he will not want to drink as much.

3. Avoid exercising the dog after he has eaten.

Enteritis

Infection or inflammation of the intestine may be caused by bacteria, poisons, worms, or the swallowing of foreign objects. Regardless of the cause, any infection or inflammation of the intestinal tract is called enteritis. This condition is usually accompanied by diarrhea or foul-smelling stools. Enteritis may cause the dog much discomfort, resulting in his assuming a prayerlike position when at rest. Enteritis may indicate a serious ailment such as parvovirus. Almost all intestinal ailments require professional care, so if these symptoms appear, contact your veterinarian immediately.

Tonsillitis

Tonsillitis, an inflammation of the tonsils, is usually caused by an oral infection. A dog with tonsillitis may run a high fever, refuse to eat, drool, and vomit frequently and violently. This ailment is also seen in dogs that have contracted distemper, hepatitis, and leptospirosis. Your veterinarian can treat it with antibiotics; only rarely is surgery required.

Respiratory Ailments

Dogs, like people, can contract the most common respiratory ailments, including coughs, asthma, bronchitis, laryngitis, and pneumonia. It is believed that dogs do not suffer from what we call the common cold. However, they do get a similar upper-respiratory infection. The symptoms include runny nose, thin mucus discharge from the eyes, slight fever, chills, coughing, and sneezing.

At one time pneumonia was a common killer of dogs because this respiratory condition so often accompanied canine distemper virus infection. However, now that most dogs are vaccinated against this disease, we find that many, if not most, cases of pneumonia are caused by bacteria that often respond to aggressive antibiotic therapy and good nursing care. Pneumonia is characterized by a rough, hacking cough, shallow breathing, nasal discharge, loss of appetite, high fever, and a quick pulse.

Most respiratory ailments can be treated with antibiotics. Take your dog to your veterinarian if he shows signs of severe respiratory problems.

Eye Disorders

Several eye disorders are common to Golden Retrievers. Some of these ailments are caused by genetic defects. Many eye disorders require corrective surgery, and all should be brought to your veterinarian's attention. Golden Retrievers expressing these traits must not be used for breeding. Following is a description of several eye ailments of which you should be aware.

Trichiasis: Trichiasis is a general term for any condition that brings eyelashes into direct contact with the cornea. This may be caused by a spastic unrolling of the eyelids or by the rubbing of an ingrown eyelash against the eye. Trichiasis causes frequent squinting, excessive tearing, and conjunctivitis (an inflammation of the membrane that keeps the dog's eye moist).

Cataracts: When cataracts are present, part of the clear lens of the eye becomes opaque, resulting in either partial or complete loss of sight. Cataracts cause the eye to turn china blue or gray.

Progressive retinal atrophy: Progressive retinal atrophy (PRA) is a hereditary ailment that progresses for months or even years; it always leads to blindness. Therefore, make sure your Golden's pedigree is free of PRA.

Other eye ailments are found in the Golden Retriever. However, most have no visible symptoms and can be diagnosed only by an ophthalmic examination by your veterinarian.

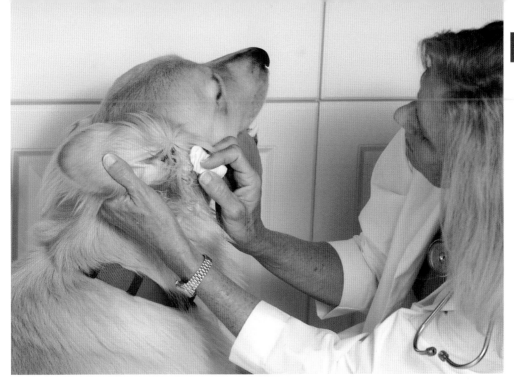

Ear Ailments

Thanks to their floppy ears, Golden Retrievers do not suffer from many ear ailments; however, one ailment they are prone to is exacerbated by this same appendage. This condition is called a hematoma, and it is characterized by blood-filled swellings in a Golden's external ear.

In general, ear problems are characterized by persistent shaking of the head, rubbing (scratching) of the ears with paws or on the floor, loss of balance, cocking the head at unusual angles, any type of discharge from the ear, or reddish inflammations in the ear.

Hematoma

When a Golden's ears are not regularly cleaned, it can lead to accumulations of wax and dirt, creating an environment that can harbor ear mites. In addition, should hair grow in the inner ears of a Golden and the area becomes damp, their long, floppy ears will not allow the inner ear to properly dry, thus making it an ideal breeding ground for bacteria. Both of these conditions will cause itching in the inner ear, and when a dog itches, he scratches. The itching and scratching can cause a blood vessel near the ear to rupture internally, which results in blood-filled swelling (hematoma) in the external ear. While these are the major causes, a hematoma can also form as the result of an injury.

When a hematoma is small it may be able to heal on its own, but it may result in the shrinking of the tissue as the swelling subsides and leaves a noticeable scar. When treating hematoma, you must also treat the source of the problem. For example, treat the ear mite infestation, or use antibiotics to fight the bacterial infection as prescribed by your veterinarian. Your veterinarian may also recommend additional medications to provide relief from the irritation and itching.

If the hematoma is large enough it can block the ear canal, preventing some medications from being administered properly. In these cases, it may require surgery to remove the clot and assure that there is no resulting disconfiguration.

Other Disorders

Hip Dysplasia

This inherited (and sometimes environmentally influenced) developmental disorder of the hip joints occurs most commonly in large breeds, including Golden Retrievers. The condition itself is due to a hip socket malformation that does not allow for the proper fit of the head of the femur.

At birth the hip of the afflicted dog appears normal, and signs of a problem may not be seen until the dog is at least five to nine months old. Hip dysplasia results in painful inflammation of the hip joint, which leads to permanent physical damage, including lameness and loss of the use of the back legs. Overfeeding, over-exercising, and injury to a puppy may also contribute to a young Golden Retriever damaging his hips.

Treatment for this ailment is to surgically correct the shape of the hip socket, or to

TIP

OFA Certification

As I have mentioned earlier in this book, insist on buying a puppy from parents that have been certified by the Orthopedic Foundation for Animals (OFA) to be clear of hip dysplasia. If you cannot get such assurance before you buy the puppy, then look elsewhere!

perform a total hip replacement. Unfortunately, these surgeries (which have a very high success rate) are performed by only a small number of specialists, so they can be quite costly. If you are planning to breed your dog, be sure to have it certified free of hereditary hip dysplasia by the OFA.

Elbow Dysplasia

This ailment is normally seen in fast-growing puppies of large breeds, and is not a simple condition to explain or understand. Elbow dysplasia is a syndrome of one or more several conditions including arthritis and malformations of the elbow joint. It is not normally seen until a puppy is six to nine months old. Symptoms include obvious limping, holding the leg out from the body when walking, or trying to walk without putting any weight on the front legs. Goldens with this condition have symptoms that become less severe as the dog matures; however, as the dog continues to mature there will most likely be permanent arthritic changes to the joint. A dog with elbow dysplasia can be made more comfortable

using oral or injectable medications, and for some dogs surgery may be recommended by your veterinarian. While this surgery has been totally successful in eliminating the problem for some dogs, depending on the severity of the dysplasia, it may continue to be a lifelong problem.

False Pregnancy

False pregnancies are caused by imbalances in the hormone levels, which control the functions of the reproductive organs. In most cases, false pregnancies do not present physical danger, although the accompanying behavioral changes can create problems.

A female behaves very similar during a false pregnancy as she would during a real one. She creeps off by herself, runs around restlessly, and paws at her bed. She also tends to carry toys, stuffed animals, or an old shoe to her bed, and defends them as if they were puppies. The biggest problem is that sometimes she may become overly aggressive in protecting her "offspring."

Usually, this condition disappears by itself, and the female returns to normal behavior. If it occurs several times a year, take your female to your veterinarian. Although hormone therapy relieves the signs of false pregnancy, it is rarely recommended because it may cause further complications.

Your veterinarian may suggest the surgical removal of the ovaries and uterus. This is safe and will save your female a great deal of pain and may even prolong her life. Removal of the ovaries and uterus also prevents recurrence of the condition, which can lead to uterine infections. This procedure should not be performed while the symptoms of false pregnancy are still apparent, however, because the protective behavior may persist. Postpone surgery until all symptoms have disappeared.

Shock

Shock is a serious condition that results from a traumatic or emotional experience. The most common causes are automobile accidents and heatstroke. A dog in shock may appear asleep, or he may be semiconscious. Symptoms vary according to the severity of the condition. Breathing may be shallow, the dog's body may be cold, and his pulse may be rapid and weak.

If your dog is in shock, try to calm him in a soft voice, pet him reassuringly, and if possible, cover him with a blanket or an article of clothing. Because the actions of a dog in shock are unpredictable, use caution in handling him. Take him to a veterinarian immediately.

Broken bones also frequently result from automobile accidents. A dog with a fracture will be in severe pain. Therefore, always remember to approach an injured dog very carefully, as he may attempt to bite you. If a dog has a compound fracture (one in which the broken bone punctures the skin), cover the wound with gauze or a clean cloth to help prevent infections. Your veterinarian will treat the fracture either by using a splint, a cast, or by surgically repairing the fracture with special orthopedic pins, or bone plates and screws.

Poisoning

Humans and dogs live their lives surrounded by poisons and toxins. Dogs, however, cannot read warning labels, which puts them at an extreme disadvantage. Most cases of dog poisoning are the result of ingestion, and on rare occasions through inhalation or absorption through the skin. Unfortunately, despite the best intentions of their owners, poisoning is common in dogs due to their curious nature and indiscriminating taste. The amount of damage a poison does is related to the amount the dog ingests (or inhales or absorbs) and how long it has been in the body before treatment. If treatment is immediate, some poisons will not have any effect, while others, regardless of the speed in which the treatment is administered, can be fatal or result in permanent damage.

The effect of a poison may not always be seen immediately. Some poisons will not cause illness for a few days to a week or more, but most common poisons result in symptoms that can be seen within three to four days of exposure. Because of this time lapse, you should never wait if you see your Golden ingesting any potentially harmful substance. If you see your dog ingest anything he should not, read the label for warnings and the proper therapy or antidote you should use. You can call your veterinarian and/or poison control center (whose phone numbers you should always have on your telephone) for the recommended course of treatment. Taking immediate action can sometimes mean the difference between life and death, so there may be some times where you will need to take action yourself. Be sure to report all toxic ingestions to your veterinarian as soon as possible.

Some of the most common poisons found in people's homes include antifreeze, acetaminophen, pesticides, and lead-based paints. Fortunately, most of these have known antidotes, but not all poisons do. Be sure to keep all potentially harmful substances away from your pets, and be sure your Golden is not in the area when you are using them.

Saying Good-bye

The most difficult time you may have to face as a pet owner occurs when your loving and loyal friend becomes terminally ill and will soon die. Although modern veterinary medicine has many ways to extend your pet's life, you must be aware that no dog will live forever. You should realize also that in some cases veterinary care can serve no useful purpose. If your dog is terminally ill and is experiencing severe and constant pain, aggressive medical attention will not extend life but rather will only prolong the dying process.

Euthanasia is the act by which a veterinarian painlessly induces death, ending the suffering of a terminally ill animal. When you must make the painful decision to have your dog put to sleep, consider the animal's feelings as well as your own. This is never an easy choice. Nevertheless, it has been made in the past by millions of pet owners who loved their friends and companions as much as you love yours. A caring veterinarian will understand the choices you may have to make and will be supportive and open to discussion. Keep in mind, however, that no one else can tell you what to do, and the decision must ultimately be made by you alone.

It is very important that when administering any medication or performing any nursing function, you are not dealing with a tense dog. Therefore, before performing these procedures becomes necessary, you should train your dog to remain calm, sit on command, and allow himself to have his mouth opened, to have his ears, eyes, and feet checked, and to be gently prodded and squeezed.

The Convalescent Dog

The recovering patient will need a warm, dry, comfortable bed. He will also need free access to his "toilet" area, even if it means carrying your dog there several times a day.

Because a dog's body temperature can drop when he is sick, be sure he is kept warm at all times. After consulting with your veterinarian, you may also want to put a luke-warm, insulated hot water bottle in your Golden's bed.

Sick dogs often become finicky eaters; however, it is extremely important that a dog eat an ample quantity of highly nutritious meals if he is to recover properly. Because a dog's appetite is stimulated by smell, you can try warming the food to between room and body temperature. This will release the odor of the food and stimulate the dog's taste buds. You should also avoid feeding a sick dog foods that may cause diarrhea whenever possible.

Goldens that are restricted in their movements may also get bedsores. Dress the affected areas (usually the elbows) with softening skin cream.

Restraining Your Golden

Should you need to perform any nursing procedure by yourself, you must know the proper way to hold and restrain your patient. This technique may also prove invaluable when grooming your Golden.

Lay the dog's head in the crook of your arm and hold it firmly, leaving your other arm free. If someone else can help you, lay the dog on his side and have the other person hold onto both the front and hind legs. While you do this, be sure to talk quietly to your Golden to help calm and reassure him.

Taking Your Dog's Temperature

In order to take your Golden's temperature, you will need a digital rectal thermometer and a jar of petroleum jelly. Because you take the dog's temperature rectally, you may need someone to help you.

Administering Eardrops

Goldens that suffer from chronic ear problems should have their ears routinely cleaned with wax-dissolving

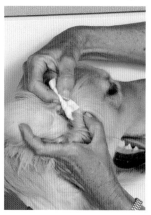

drops. First lift the flap of the ear and clean away any visible wax with a cotton ball moistened with a wax-removal solution provided by your veterinarian. With the ear flap laid back, insert the nozzle of the bottle in the ear in a forward direction (toward the tip of the nose). Squeeze the proper amount of drops into the ear, being sure to hold the dog's head still during the entire process. Then, without letting the dog shake his head, gently massage the ear to lubricate the entire ear canal with medication.

SICK DOG

The normal body temperature of an adult Golden Retriever is between 101.5° and 102.5°F (38–39.2°C). The temperature is slightly higher in younger dogs and slightly lower in older ones. If your dog is placid, simply lubricate the thermometer with petroleum jelly, lift the dog's tail, and slip the thermometer in. You can remove it after two or three minutes. If your dog is restless, have someone else calm him and hold his head firmly as previously described. Then lift his tail and insert the thermometer. Wash the thermometer in cold water when you are done.

An elevated temperature is often a sign of fever, infection, pain, stress, or just excitement. A temperature below normal (hypothermia) may indicate a debilitating disease, disorder, or poisoning.

Taking a Pulse

You should also learn to take your dog's pulse. It is best to feel the pulse on the inside of the thigh. An adult Golden has a pulse rate of 70 to 90 beats per minute, whereas in younger dogs it is slightly faster. In a calm, healthy Golden, the pulse is strong and steady. A weak pulse may indicate poisoning or shock, whereas an irregular, pounding pulse may be a symptom of fever or infection.

Administering Medicines

Powdered medications can be mixed with water and, like liquid medications, drawn into a syringe without a needle on it. Open the lips in the back of your dog's mouth near his molars, and slowly squirt the liquid as far back into his throat as possible.

Your dog may refuse to take a pill by itself. Put the medication inside some meat. Make sure your dog swallows all the medicine. Some dogs very cleverly hide pills in their mouths and spit them out when the owner's back is turned. You

may have to force your dog to swallow a pill. Hold the dog's upper jaw and, exerting mild pressure, raise his head. This should cause the dog's mouth to open. Quickly place the pill on the back of his tongue, hold his mouth closed, and tilt his head upward. This will force your dog to swallow the pill.

Applying Eyedrops

Be sure to first clean the eyes with moistened cotton by gently softening and then wiping away the debris from the corners of the eyes. Using an eyewash solution provided by your veterinarian, irrigate the eye with moistened cotton, being careful not to get any cotton fibers on the eye itself. Then, gently restrain the dog and hold the eye open. So as not to frighten the dog, bring the bottle to the eye from above and behind. Gently squeeze the proper number of drops into the eye and allow the medication time to bathe the eye before releasing your restraint on the patient.

Eye ointments should be applied in a line along the lower lid (being sure not to let the applicator touch the eye). Hold the dog's eye closed for a few seconds so that the ointment warms and disperses.

BASIC AND ADVANCED TRAINING

Like most hunting dogs, the Golden Retriever is relatively easy to train. Several hundred years of close hunter-retriever relationships have given this breed a strong desire and willingness to learn.

Golden Retrievers truly excel in training. Because they love human companionship, you can begin training them much earlier than many other breeds. In addition, if you conduct your training program properly, you will be able to keep your Golden puppy's attention for a longer period, thus leading to quicker learning.

Even if you do not plan to enter your dog in field or obedience trials, you should still teach him the skills for which his breed was developed. This includes any of the retrieving and hurdling exercises.

Bear in mind that this chapter does not describe all the skills a Golden can learn. In fact, I believe that if you have the time, patience, and energy, you can teach your Golden an endless number of skills. You must, however, be able to communicate your ideas to your eager student.

Because they learn rapidly, if taught properly Goldens are extremely obedient. Goldens, along with German Shepherds and Labrador Retrievers, dominate the guide dog (Seeing Eye) field. This trainability has made the Golden Retriever one of the top breeds competing in field and obedience trials.

Basic Rules of Training

Each time you hold a training session for your Golden, consider the following points:

1. You and your family must be consistent. All household members must decide what is permitted and what is prohibited. Once you have taught your dog a lesson, never allow him to do the contrary without reprimand.

2. Be authoritative. Although your dog must learn that you are in charge, never do this by using physical force. Goldens can quickly learn

5. Praise your dog thoroughly after he has performed correctly. Verbal praise and petting or scratching behind the ears will make your Golden an eager learner. Although I am not a believer in giving food rewards as a form of praise, there are times when it can be used to help encourage a dog to learn particularly difficult commands. In the case of training your dog to relinquish an object, it can really cut down the learning curve.

6. Disobedience must be dealt with immediately. Because puppies have a very short memory, never hesitate to reprimand them. If your puppy chews a slipper, do not reprimand him unless you catch him in the act. An adult Golden, on the other hand, most certainly would know right from wrong, and can be shown the shredded evidence before being punished. For both puppies and adults, punishment should never be in the form of physical violence but instead should consist of verbal disapproval. In extreme cases, you can confine the culprit to his crate after issuing a verbal reprimand.

7. Begin working with your puppy the day you bring him home. Hold two or three sessions a day, and continue these sessions as long as your puppy shows interest. Limit your sessions to 10 or 15 minutes each to provide sufficient teaching without boring your dog. Your puppy may need two weeks or longer to begin to understand some of your commands, so do not neglect your training. Goldens must learn these basic lessons at a young age.

Why Dogs Learn

Dogs are instinctively pack animals. Because they hunt and live as a group, dogs must learn to coexist with each other in order to survive. This coexistence depends on ranking order.

hand signals, and they can understand sounds. Therefore, make all visual and verbal commands clearly and unambiguously. Because dogs understand tones better than words, be sure your reprimands are always sharp and firm while your praise is always calm and friendly.

3. Run each training session with an atmosphere conducive to learning. Have your dog perform the lesson where there are as few distractions as possible. In addition, never attempt to teach a puppy anything if you are in a bad mood. This will only confuse the puppy and make learning harder.

4. Do not attempt to teach your dog more than one concept in a single training session, and never move on to another concept until your dog has mastered the previous lesson. Puppies, like people, learn at their own pace and should never be rushed.

Each dog has a place in the ranking order, usually based on strength and experience. In the pack, all dogs submit to a dog of higher authority. Similarly, a domesticated dog submits only to a higher ranking authority.

Through training, a puppy learns that you are his master and that the other members of your family rank higher than he does. In addition to establishing ranking order, training teaches your puppy the rules of your house. Teaching a puppy actions and behaviors that are not instinctive takes patience, understanding, and love. You must be consistent and authoritative, yet must never lose your temper. Try to understand that human ways are unfamiliar to your Golden puppy, but that he is eager to learn. Your puppy depends on you to find the proper way to teach him. Once you find the right method, your puppy will respond eagerly and joyfully.

Training a Puppy

As previously mentioned, training begins the day you bring your puppy home. The longer you wait, the more difficult it will be for your puppy to learn. First teach your Golden his name. If you always address your puppy using his name, you will be amazed at how fast he will learn this lesson. Make sure your Golden does not hear nicknames; this will confuse him, and he will not respond when called.

Another important lesson is the meaning of *"No."* Your puppy will probably have to begin learning this lesson his first day at home. As your puppy first explores your home, he will probably do something wrong. When he does, tell him *"No"* in a sharp, firm tone that shows you are serious. If your puppy refuses to listen, pick him up and place him in his crate. *Never*

hit your puppy, either with your hand or with a rolled newspaper, for this will make your puppy hand-shy. Using a crate will simplify training. In addition, as you will see in the next section, it will also speed the process of housebreaking.

Walking on a Leash

From the very first time you walk your puppy, begin to teach him how to walk on a leash. Place a collar on the puppy, making sure it is neither loose enough to slip over the head or tight enough to restrict breathing. Attach a leash and

take your puppy for his first walk. Teach your puppy to walk on your left side. Try to keep him close to your leg, but not under your feet, and do not allow him to pull you along. Remember to be patient. If your puppy falls behind, do not attempt to drag him behind you. Keep him in his proper walking position with friendly words and a little gentle force, if necessary.

Begging Is Forbidden

Begging is a bad habit for a puppy to develop. Do not allow it to begin. If, when you sit down for a meal, your puppy starts to beg or just sits nearby, staring at you with pleading eyes, be firm. Say in a strict tone *"No!"* and

point away from the table and toward the puppy's crate or sleeping box. Within a few weeks your puppy will learn not to approach the table.

Being Alone

To accustom your puppy to being alone, leave him in a familiar room. Then go into another room where the puppy can neither see nor hear you. Stay there for a short while and then return; if your puppy has done anything wrong, reprimand him. Gradually increase the time you leave the dog in the room.

If you must leave before you can trust your puppy alone, lock him in his crate with food, water, and toys until you return. If you do not have a crate, lock him in a familiar room. Remove all tempting objects, including shoes, papers, and clothing. Make sure you leave the puppy his bed and an ample supply of food, water, and toys.

Do not leave a very young puppy alone in your yard, where there are too many uncontrollable factors. Children may tease the puppy, and other animals may bother or hurt him.

Simple Commands

The first commands to teach your puppy are *sit, stay, come,* and *heel.* Teach these commands using these words and not phrases like *"Come over here, Max."* Your puppy does not understand complete sentences, but rather relies on the command word, your tone, and your gestures. Do not try to teach your puppy these commands for long periods of time. It is better to train for short periods two or three times a day. Train your puppy before you feed him because afterwards he may be sluggish. Also, make sure to walk the dog before

training. To avoid distractions, train your puppy in a confined area without an audience.

Sit: Take your puppy into an isolated room and fit him with a collar and leash. Hold the leash with your right hand and place your left hand on the puppy's hindquarters. Then give the command *"Sit!"* or *"Sit, Max!"* in a firm voice, at the same time pressing gently and steadily on his hindquarters. Gently pull the leash upward to keep your puppy from lying down on the floor. Hold the dog in this position for a while. Do not allow him to jump back up.

Do not expect your Golden to master this command after the first training session. Repeat the procedure for the entire session or until the puppy begins to lose interest. Remember to praise his efforts each time he sits.

Once your puppy has performed the *sit* at least a couple of times in succession, remove the leash. If your dog has been properly trained, he will perform correctly. If not, remain patient and try again with the leash on.

If you want to use your Golden in the field, teach him to respond to a hand signal as well. In the field your dog may be at a distance where he can see you but not hear you. This way your dog can understand your command even if noise prevents him from hearing you. Once your puppy has mastered the command, hold up either your hand or a single finger in a distinct gesture and say *"Sit,"* making sure the dog can see the signal. Always use the word and the gesture together so your dog connects the two.

Stay: This is a more difficult command to teach your Golden, for he will always want to be at your side. The *stay* command orders your dog to remain still wherever he is. This command may someday save your dog's life.

In teaching your dog to *stay*, first fit him with a leash and collar. Then run through the *sit* procedure and follow it with the command *"Stay."* As you say this new command, raise your hand, palm toward the dog, like a police officer stopping traffic. Each time your dog attempts to stand up, reproach him with a sharp *"No!"*

Take up all the slack in the leash to hold your dog in place. Repeat the procedure until the dog appears to understand. Then remove the leash and repeat the command several times. Praise the dog each time he obeys. If he disobeys, reprimand him.

Once you have repeated this command with regular success, begin to back away from the dog slowly, always maintaining eye contact. As you back away, keep repeating the word *"Stay"* while making the proper hand gesture. If your dog attempts to follow you, give him a loud, sharp *"Stay!"* If he continues to follow you, reprimand him. If the dog stays when told, praise him greatly, for he will be very tempted to follow you.

Come: If you call your Golden puppy's name, he will probably barrel across the room to greet you. However, your dog may eventually find something that attracts his attention more than you. The objective of the command *come* is to have your dog come running whether he wants to or not.

You should teach the command *come* to your puppy right after *sit* and *stay*. Start by running through the *sit* and *stay* procedures. Once he has *stayed* at a good distance, call him by name and follow with the command *"Max, come!"* Accompany your words with a lively sound or gesture like clapping your hands or slapping your thighs. This will help excite your dog into motion.

Your Golden will quickly associate the word *"Come"* with your movements. Praise him for responding correctly. If he does not respond to the command, put him on a long rope and let him wander off. Then slowly reel in the rope while repeating the word *"Come."* Shower your dog with praise when he reaches you. Repeat this exercise several times; then try it without the rope again. *Come* is another command that can protect your dog from dangerous situations.

Housebreaking a Puppy

For obvious reasons, housebreaking a puppy has never been a lot of fun for the dog owner. There are certain methods, however, that can speed up the process and avoid a lot of the surprises associated with it.

Paper Training

The objective of paper training is to get your puppy to urinate and defecate on newspapers spread out in an area of your choosing. Kitchens and bathrooms make the best locations because they are easy to clean. The papers, however, must not be placed too close to the puppy's eating or sleeping areas, because your Golden will make every effort to keep those areas clean and will not excrete near them.

At first you can confine your puppy to the room you have chosen until he voids. If he used the paper, remove the top sheets and place fresh, clean papers under what were formerly the bottom sheets. By doing this, you will be leaving the scent from the bottom papers exposed so that the puppy can relocate the area more easily to repeat the act.

If the puppy misses the paper at first, attempt to get the scent of the dog's urine

onto a sheet of newspaper and place him on top of the other sheets. Then thoroughly clean the inappropriate area that the puppy used. It is important that the puppy seek out his scent on the papers and not find it on the floor, where he will repeat his action.

Try to remember that after eating, drinking, playing, or waking up, your Golden will probably need to empty his bladder and bowels. Young puppies need to relieve themselves every few hours. Oftentimes, the only sign your puppy will give that he needs to relieve himself is that he will begin sniffing the ground. By doing this, your Golden is actually sniffing out the place that "smells right" for him to do his duty. Some puppies may both sniff the ground and begin to run around frantically. When this happens, you have only seconds to react, by picking up your puppy and placing him on the newspaper in the designated area of your home. You can then gently restrain the puppy's movements until he has relieved himself on the paper.

It is important to praise the puppy after he has "gone" on the paper.

Crate Training

Crate training offers an easier and faster alternative to paper training and takes advantage of the fact that your puppy will instinctively try to keep his sleeping area clean. If your puppy is wary on his first encounter with the crate, make it more appealing by placing some toys inside for your pet to play with. After you have confined the puppy to his crate a few times with his excreta, he will quickly learn to restrain himself until you let him out of the crate. Of course, after you release the puppy from his crate, you must take him outdoors immediately. Establish a time schedule for him to relieve himself before bringing him back indoors. As your trust in your puppy grows, you can let him out for longer and longer periods until, eventually, you can leave the crate door open at all times without fear

of "accidents," provided that you take the dog outside as scheduled.

Using a crate also has additional benefits. Before domestication, dogs were cave-dwelling animals. Instinctively, the modern dog finds security in any cavelike structure once he becomes familiar with it. If you choose to use a crate, you will find that your dog will actually prefer to sleep there and will return on his own. In addition to its use in housebreaking, a crate, therefore, can serve as a sleeping box and a traveling crate and can also prove helpful when you are unable to supervise the puppy.

The crate can also serve as an invaluable training tool. Should your puppy refuse to listen to your commands, you can pick him up and put him in his crate. Isolating your Golden from your presence is one of the best ways of letting him know that you are unhappy with his performance.

Outdoor Training

Outdoor training begins when you first bring your puppy home. Before taking him indoors, walk him to the area you have chosen where

he is to eliminate. Give your Golden plenty of time to relieve himself, and praise him thoroughly when he is done. Verbal praise and petting will reinforce your puppy's confidence and will increase the chances of a successful repeat performance later on.

Because most puppies have to relieve themselves as many as six times a day, you should take your pet outdoors about once every three or four hours. It is also advisable to walk the puppy after every one of his meals. When a puppy's stomach is full, extra pressure is exerted on the bladder, so it is best not to wait too long. You should take your puppy for his last walk as late in the evening as possible, thereby increasing your Golden's chances of making it through the night without accidents. If you continue to bring your puppy to the same area each time and praise him for each successful performance, he will eventually seek out this area on his own.

Cleaning Up

Although canine droppings are aesthetically unpleasant, you should always clean up after your dog. Because these droppings can be considered a minor health hazard, many towns and cities have made it illegal *not* to clean up after your pet.

Whenever you walk your dog, carry a plastic bag or "pooper-scooper" with you and dispose of the mess in its proper place. When cleaning your garden or yard, it is actually best to flush the mess down the toilet, as roundworms and tapeworms can be transmitted in the feces. For those "accidents" that happen in the home, clean with an odor-eliminating disinfectant. Do not use ammonia because the smell will remind your puppy of his urine.

Accidents Will Happen

No matter which method of housebreaking you choose for your puppy, it is inevitable that "accidents" will eventually occur. If you discover that while you slept your puppy could no longer control himself, it will do no good to administer punishment. Puppies have very short memories, so if you do not catch your puppy in the act, or make the discovery shortly afterward, a scolding will only confuse your pet. Should you catch your Golden in the act, rebuke him with a sharp *"No!"* and then put him in his crate. Never spank your puppy, and never put the puppy's nose in the mess. Not only is this an unsanitary thing to do, but also it may well upset the puppy to the point that you will have one more thing to clean up.

Obedience Training

Heeling

When a dog *heels,* he walks at your left side with his head level with your knees. Your Golden should learn to *heel* first on a leash, and eventually to walk correctly without restraint.

To start, run through the commands your dog has already mastered. This will give your dog confidence before starting this difficult lesson. Firmly grasp your dog's leash with your left hand about halfway toward his collar, enabling you to guide him. Walk briskly and give the command *"Heel!"* or *"Heel, Max!"* in a sharp tone of voice. At first your dog will probably act unpredictably. He may bolt ahead, pull back, or even jump about in an effort to play.

If your dog lags behind, pull steadily on the leash to bring him even with your leg. Do not

drag the dog forward or force him to obey your commands, for this will destroy your well-established learning atmosphere. If your dog runs forward, pull him back to your side and give the *heel* command again. If you have difficulty getting your dog to perform correctly, run him through the old *sit* and *stay* exercises. Whenever your dog responds correctly, praise him. When he reacts improperly, reprimand him immediately. When he has performed the *sit* and *stay* correctly, begin the *heel* exercises again.

Do not try to teach your dog to heel too quickly. This lesson usually takes a long time

and much patience. Once your dog has mastered the heel on the leash, take him through a turning exercise. If he has trouble heeling while you turn, take a shorter grip on the leash to persuade him to turn as you do. As you do this, repeat the command *"Heel!"* in a sharp tone. Once your dog begins to learn, walk him through a series of straight line, right turn, and left turn exercises. When he has mastered turning, begin training on a slack leash.

Go through the heeling exercises with the leash exerting no pressure on your dog's collar. At the dog's first mistake, grasp the leash firmly and lead the dog steadily in the proper direction. When he performs correctly, remember to praise him.

When your dog has learned to walk correctly with a slack leash, remove the leash completely. If your dog reverts to bad habits, immediately reprimand him with a sharp *"No!"*

If necessary, put the leash back on. Then run through the *heel* lessons and try again without the leash. It is very important to remember to praise your dog whenever he performs an exercise properly to reinforce his good behavior.

Relinquishing an Object

This is usually easy for Golden Retrievers to learn, for they are not as possessive as some other breeds. Start by giving your dog a ball or a suitably sized piece of nonsplintering wood to hold in his teeth. Then command the dog to sit, praising him once he obeys the command. Slowly pull the dog's jaws apart with both hands and say *"Let go!"* strictly and firmly. If he begins to growl, tell him *"No!"* Do not be afraid if your dog growls, for this is his natural reaction to anyone who attempts to take away his prey. Rarely will a Golden do more than growl.

If you are having trouble teaching your star pupil this command, it may be time to consider using a food reward, which should be healthy. If your Golden is demonstrating too much possessiveness of the object he has retrieved, offering one of his favorite treats in exchange will probably get him to immediately drop the ball and look to get the treat. If this happens, place the object back in his mouth, use the command *"Let Go!,"* and while holding the treat out with one hand, use the other to take the object out. Be sure to use verbal praise and then the treat can be turned over to your eager pupil.

Lying Down

Start by having your dog sit. Then slowly pull his front legs forward, push down on his shoulders, and command him firmly by saying *"Down."* Carefully step on the leash to prevent the dog from returning to his feet. Keep the dog in this position for about one minute. Gradually increase the time period as your dog progresses. When your dog begins to lie down on his own, begin to walk away from him while maintaining constant eye contact. Whenever the dog attempts to stand up, repeat the command *"Down"* in a firm, sharp tone.

Training for Hunting Dogs

Retrieving

Retrieving will obviously come fairly naturally to a Golden. Simply throw a stick or a ball, with your dog standing next to you, and call out *"Fetch."* Your Golden will probably go after the object and return it to you. Command the dog to sit, put out your hand, palm up, under his lower jaw, and say, *"Let go!"* You should be able to remove the object from the dog's mouth without any resistance. If your dog drops the object on the ground, place it back into his mouth, and then remove it, saying *"Let go!"* If your Golden shows no desire to return with the object, repeat the exercise using a 30-foot (9-m)

rope. Tie the dog to the cord, throw the object, and call out *"Fetch!"* again. Once he has picked up the object, draw the dog toward you. Then take the object from him.

Jumping Over Hurdles

Because Goldens truly enjoy jumping, they learn this lesson with relative ease. First, command your dog to sit on one side of a small pile of boards, while you stand on the opposite side. Command the dog by saying *"Jump!"* If he walks around the obstacle, say *"No!,"* then bring him back and start over. Praise your dog for a successful performance.

As your dog learns to jump over the hurdle on command, gradually increase the obstacle's height. Be careful not to make the jump too high, for this can hurt young dogs and discourage further jumping.

Once your dog has learned to jump on command, begin a jump and retrieve exercise. Place the object to be retrieved on the other side of the hurdle. Command your dog to sit next to you. Then command him to retrieve the object by saying *"Jump! Fetch!"* in a clear, firm voice. The dog should leap over the obstacle, pick up the object, and jump back with it. Tell the dog to sit again. Then take the object out of his mouth by saying *"Let go!"* Praise your dog warmly for his accomplishments.

Golden Retrievers in Competition

Many Golden owners are attracted to participating in dog shows, because it combines the excitement of competition with a chance to spend more quality time with their dogs. In the United States the AKC sponsors many events that attract millions of participants. These events include conformation shows, obedience trials, field trials, hunting tests, agility trials, Canine Good Citizen tests, lure coursing, herding trials, and tracking tests. While Golden Retrievers can compete in many of these events, they are most commonly found competing in conformance shows, obedience trials, field trials, and hunting tests that are designed for dogs that have been bred as hunting companions.

Should you decide to try the show ring, keep in mind that no individual dog can please everyone. While it would be great if your Golden delighted each judge he met, you should not count on this happening, for dogs of that caliber are extremely rare. It is much more important that your dog pleases you. Never blame your dog for failure in the ring, for if it were up to your Golden, he would win every award possible to please you. Go to the shows, have a good time, and learn all you can. Afterward, bring your beloved companion back home and show him that you still believe that he is the best dog in the world.

Conformation Events

Conformation events are shows in which the quality of the breeding stock is evaluated, so spayed or neutered dogs cannot compete in these events. In these shows, a Golden would be judged on his appearance, physique, bearing, temperament, and how well the dog conforms to the breed standard.

There are three types of conformation dog shows: all-breed shows, specialty shows for a specific breed, and group shows, which are limited to dogs belonging to one of the seven AKC groups (Working, Herding, Sporting, Non-sporting, Hounds, Terrier, and Toy). Naturally, Goldens would compete in the Sporting group. The AKC also offers children between the ages of 9 and 18 the opportunity to compete in junior showmanship events. Here, the juniors are judged on how well they present their dogs.

If you are interested and want to know more about conformation shows, you can start by joining a local kennel club that will have information on training classes for the show ring. You should also attend a show as a visitor. If the grooming area is open to the public, talk to professional groomers to get some tips. If you are considering the purchase of a Golden, you will have the opportunity to talk to many expert breeders and exhibitors. You can also find pet product vendors and club booths that

often offer helpful information. Once you know what to expect, you can better enjoy the experience of competitive dog shows.

Obedience Trials

Goldens are a superlative-performing breed in the obedience ring. There are three levels of training in which a dog can compete for an obedience title: Novice, Open, and Utility. These trials are open to all registered dogs over the age of six months that are qualified, by training, to participate.

• Novice class dogs usually have had at least one year of training in following practical commands used in everyday living such as *heel* (both with and without a leash), *come*, and *stay*.

• Open level is more stringent, and includes exercises such as retrieving and jumping hurdles.

• Utility level is the class for the best of the best, and includes scent discrimination and silent signaling.

Novice dogs compete to earn a Companion Dog (CD) title. Open level is the class in which dogs compete for the Companion Dog Excellent (CDX) title. The top honor of Utility Dog (UD) is given to the best in the utility class.

The AKC also has non-title classes that the beginning obedience handler and dog can enter to prepare for the titled ones. Most competitors start by taking obedience classes as a way of gaining control over their pets, but find that working with their dogs can be a very rewarding experience. If you are interested in finding out more, the AKC website provides a list of scheduled events as well as a copy of the AKC Obedience Regulations.

Field Trials

Working in the field with a Golden is one of the greatest feelings a hunter can experience. Goldens are retrieving dogs, and their purpose in the field is to retrieve downed birds. Because they are specialized, there are separate field trials that were devised specifically for retrievers. A field trial is designed to see how well a dog

perfoms his hunting duties against an established standardized platform. During field trials, the competing dogs will need to follow a hunter's voice commands and hand signals from a distance as they guide them through a land and water course to find "downed" birds to bring back to their master. The AKC has published specific field trial rules and procedures for retrievers, which you can find on their website.

Agility Trials

Agility competitions have become more and more popular each year. It is truly a sport for those energetic owners who want to have fun

obstacles such as climbing and descending an A-frame, traversing an elevated dog walk, and crossing a see-saw, or the AKC Jumpers with Weaves Class, which involves jumps, tunnels, and weave poles. Both classes offer increasing levels of difficulty as the dogs compete to win a Novice, Open, Excellent, or Master title.

For those who have never seen an agility competition, I strongly urge you to attend one in your area, as the excitement that the top dog/handler teams can generate is unparalleled in the competition ring.

Problems in Training

Remember that all Golden Retrievers are different. Each has its idiosyncrasies, and learning abilities vary greatly. I have found that more than half the battle is establishing the proper rapport with your dog. All the training exercises described in this chapter are no more than outlines for teaching commands. As your dog's trainer, you must establish an appropriate communication system in which your dog will understand what you want him to perform.

✔ If your dog shows an unwillingness to learn a lesson, remain calm and understanding. Never force your Golden to learn. Anger and beatings have *never* helped a dog learn anything. Such actions only create an atmosphere inconducive to learning, and cause your dog to lose his trust in you.

✔ If your dog does not seem to be learning a particular lesson, examine your teaching methods. Review the section on basic rules of training and review each of the seven points listed. Ask yourself if you have followed these points during all of your training sessions.

✔ In most cases, the fault lies in the owner's teaching methods. If you feel, however, that this

with their Goldens. Not only will it help create a lasting bond between the dog and owner, it will also help keep you both in shape. In agility trials, both the dog and handler need to run at full speed while performing exercises both accurately and safely. Dogs can compete in either the AKC Standard Class, which includes is not the problem, then carefully examine your dog and his environment. Are you holding your lessons where your dog is being distracted by an outside force, or is your dog ill? If you suspect illness, bring your dog to your veterinarian.

✔ If you continue to have difficulty training your dog, contact your Golden Retriever Club and/or a highly recommended obedience school. These facilities have professional dog handlers who can examine your training regimen and help you identify problems.

✔ If you are diligent and establish a harmonious learning atmosphere for your dog, you and your faithful four-legged friend will enjoy many wonderful years of camaraderie.

Obedience Schools Can Help

Obedience schools are not schools for "wayward" dogs, but rather a place where you can learn all the exercises needed to compete in shows. Even if you are not planning to enter your dog in a show, obedience schools offer an enjoyable and interesting alternative to training your dog alone. In addition, it also makes training easier, as you will work under the guidance of an experienced dog handler.

If you have an older child, let him or her take your Golden to obedience classes. This will allow child and dog to spend more time together. It also teaches your child how to take responsibility for the care of a pet. Working with an obedience school will teach your child greater respect for both the dog and himself/herself.

Check with your local Golden Retriever Club and the AKC for a reputable obedience school in your area. Before enrolling your dog, be sure the class suits your purpose. Most schools offer special classes for owners interested in showing their dogs, and others offer classes for amateurs.

Guide Dog Training

Goldens are friendly, obedient, patient, and easy to train. Their body size and almost maintenance-free coat make them ideal guide dogs. Goldens trained as Seeing Eye dogs are selected by experts who determine that the dogs have all necessary qualifications.

All guide dogs must be trustworthy and friendly to all people, patient, and totally obedient. Guide dogs usually begin their training at the age of one year. Guide dogs must learn that there is no room for error, for mistakes can mean serious harm to their masters.

There are basic differences between guide dog and regular training. Guide dogs are trained to take the lead and to show initiative. They must learn to work with a harness, and learn to avoid obstacles.

Although all Golden Retrievers possess many of the requirements needed to be guide dogs, not all of them have all the necessary physical, temperamental, and mental characteristics. Only exceptionally talented dogs are chosen for this duty.

UNDERSTANDING THE GOLDEN RETRIEVER

The Golden Retriever is an extremely complex creature. To understand their behavior patterns, we must take a close look at the process by which dogs evolved, became domesticated, and were selectively bred to create the pure breed we know today.

Origins and Early History

The development of the Golden Retriever began in the 19th century with the very careful planning and dedication of an Englishman, Sir Dudley Marjoriebanks, the first Lord of Tweedmouth. Lord Tweedmouth lived on an estate in Scotland, where he did a great deal of hunting. His fondness for hunting led him to search for the perfect hunting dog. He attempted to reach his goal by obtaining good hunting dogs that he then outcrossed with other breeds. Outcrossing is a process by which dogs with no mutual ancestors are bred together. The purpose is to continue the special hunting traits of different breeds. Through outcrossing, Sir Dudley eventually developed a breed later known as the Golden Retriever.

The Golden Retriever was originally believed to have been the result of the crossbreeding of Russian tracking dogs and Bloodhounds. This was still believed in the early 1950s. In 1952, however, the original Stud Book of Lord Tweedmouth was made available for study by his great nephew, the sixth Earl of Ilchester. The Stud Book was a detailed record of all Lord Tweedmouth's breeding attempts in the mid- to late 19th century.

Lord Tweedmouth purchased a yellow Retriever from a cobbler in Brighton in 1865. The dog, named Nous, was the only yellow in a litter of black Wavy-coated Retrievers. Black Wavy-coats, the predecessors of today's Flat-coated Retrievers, were developed from crosses of lesser Newfoundlands and several types of setters. Lesser Newfoundlands were an early American breed and should not be confused with present-day Newfoundlands.

The female bred with Nous was a Tweed Water Spaniel named Belle. This breed is now extinct, and its exact origins are unknown. We do know, however, that early Water Spaniels were a cross between various spaniels and early water dogs. Water Spaniels were known for their superior retrieving abilities, high intelligence, and excellent swimming skills.

The litter of Nous and Belle consisted of four females—Ada, Primrose, Crocus, and Cowslip. Although all were very important to Lord Tweedmouth, records indicate that Cowslip had the greatest number of traits that he deemed desirable for the development of the perfect hunting retriever.

Lord Tweedmouth's plan was to carefully line-breed all his dogs back to Cowslip. Linebreeding means breeding a female to a dog that has the same ancestors (although it is not directly related). First, Lord Tweedmouth obtained another Tweed Water Spaniel and bred it to Cowslip. From this litter, he took a female puppy and later bred her to a descendant of Ada. He performed this type of linebreeding for several generations. In order to reduce the risks of excessive linebreeding, however, he made several outcrosses. He introduced black Wavy-coated Retrievers to the line in order to improve hunting abilities. He added an Irish Setter—another hunting dog—in order to improve the breed's color. Finally, he used a sandy-colored Bloodhound to increase tracking ability and to insure color.

Today's Golden Retriever is the result of very selective linebreeding for type and planned outcrossing for ability and color. Lord Tweedmouth's dedicated work produced the original line of Golden Retrievers, the Ilchesters. In 1903, the Kennel Club of England first registered the Golden Retriever under the category "Flat-Coats-Golden." In 1911, the Kennel Club recognized Goldens as a separate breed called "Yellow or Golden Retrievers." A few years later "Yellow" was dropped from the name, and the breed became known officially as the Golden Retriever.

The Golden Retriever in the United States

The archives of the Golden Retriever Club of America (GRCA) record Goldens in the United States as early as the 1890s. However, no serious breeding was documented until the 1930s. In 1933, Colonel Samuel Magoffin showed a Golden import named Speedwell Pluto. That year the dog won Best In Show at Puget Sound, Washington, the first time a Golden won this honor in the United States.

The AKC officially recognized the Golden Retriever in 1932, although registrations of the breed had been accepted earlier. In 1938, the Golden Retriever Club of America was formed; its first president was Colonel Magoffin. Today the GRCA is one of the largest parent breed clubs in the United States. Its purpose is to advance and protect the Golden in all aspects of life—whether as show dog, hunting dog, or family companion. If you are interested in Goldens, by all means join the GRCA. It will prove a valuable source of help and information regarding nearly all your dog's needs.

The Nature of the Golden Retriever

Now that we have examined the origins of the Golden, you can see how it acquired its

size, shape, and color. To understand the Golden's behavior patterns, however, we must examine the process by which dogs evolved and were domesticated. All dogs, regardless of breed, trace their ancestry to a form of wild dog or wolf.

Basic Instincts

As previously mentioned, wild dogs have a specially structured society. Most of their behavior rituals allow each member of the pack to live in harmony with the others. With the passing of many, many generations of dogs, some of these rituals became instinctive. Modern domesticated dogs will exhibit many of these instinctive behavior patterns, including marking of territory and establishing a ranking order among human companions.

Compared with most other breeds, the Golden Retriever appears not to possess as many instinctive behavior patterns. For example, Goldens rarely exhibit such survival instincts as fighting spirit, possessiveness over food, or the urge to protect its home or itself. The Golden may mark its territory; however, it will not defend it with the zeal of a German Shepherd, for example.

It is believed that dogs were the first domesticated animal; evidence indicates that this process began about 12,000 years ago. Humans probably tamed wolves or wild dogs to assist them in hunting. Hunting practices and social structures of both humans and dogs were probably very similar at this time.

Domestication

As dogs became domestic, they lost many of their instinctive behavior patterns. Which traits were lost and which were retained depends on the specific breed and how it was domesti-

cated. As you know, Golden Retrievers were originally bred as hunting dogs. Thus, Goldens naturally display excellent hunting and tracking skills.

Because Goldens and their domestic ancestors were all hunting dogs, they received a great deal of human contact. Dogs used as retrievers must undergo substantial training by a hunter. This relationship turns the dog into a companion, as well as a hunting tool. More than any other factor, this training is probably responsible for the people-oriented nature of the Golden Retriever.

The gentle, friendly, obedient nature of the Golden Retriever is the result of generations of selective breeding. Since the mid-19th century, breeders have carefully developed the traits they deemed desirable in Goldens and have tried to eliminate unwanted behavior patterns. Thus, breeders have successfully weeded out many inherent canine behaviors that would be undesirable in hunting dogs.

In summary, the nature of the Golden Retriever is a blend of three elements. The first includes all instinctive behavior, such as sexual drive, the marking of territories, and the establishment of a ranking order. The second and third elements are a result of domestication; they include selectively bred traits and "people-oriented" traits developed from the hunter-dog relationship.

Behavior Problems

Although the Golden Retriever is renowned for ease of training, as well as a friendly nature, in recent years, accounts have been told of Goldens too hyperactive for average owners to properly train. An increasing number of reports have also been made regarding unprovoked attacks by Goldens upon other dogs and people, including their owners. Not all of these incidents are believed to be the result of poor training. The cause of these temperament problems is probably careless breeding practices, for the Golden's loving nature is the result of many years of well-planned, careful training.

Abnormal behavior patterns are practically impossible to detect in a Golden puppy. Therefore, be sure to purchase your puppy from a reliable, conscientious breeder. Even if you do this, however, your dog may still develop behavioral problems. You can control most of these abnormalities by extensive training and counterconditioning. In addition, for the sake of the breed, do not breed a Golden that exhibits behavior problems. You do not want to increase the incidence of these problems.

What Your Dog Can Tell You

All dogs use their voices, body language, and facial expressions to convey their emotions. Sometimes you must pay special attention to these characteristics in order to understand your dog's moods.

Dogs do not make noises without a reason. Each sound reflects a mood. A dog will yelp in fright or pain, whine and whimper in loneliness or when seeking attention, groan in contentment or when ailing, and bark in anger or glee. Often you must look for additional signs to determine the purpose of the sounds.

Body Language

Body language is also a good indicator of a dog's mood. A joyous dog jumps up and down eagerly and may bark. A dog that crouches and

lowers his head to the floor is exhibiting fear, either of being punished or of an intruder or another dog. The best indicator of your dog's emotions, however, is his tail. A happy dog wags his tail briskly (the happier he is, the more briskly his tail wags). A frightened dog puts his tail between his legs. An alert or attentive Golden raises his tail slightly, while a content dog has a lowered tail (but not between his legs).

Facial Expressions

Finally, watch your Golden's ears and muzzle, for they are a primary means of facial expression. A content Golden has a closed mouth and lowered ears. An alert, aroused, or attentive dog picks up his ears (only the part of the ear on the top of the Golden's head rises, not his entire ear). Often your dog will cock his head inquisitively to one side or the other. Be wary

of any dog whose ears are back, upper lips are raised, mouth is open, and who is growling. Although you will rarely—if ever—see a Golden Retriever in this position, remember that these are all warning signals of fear and/or anger, and they may precede an attack.

The Sense Organs

Dogs in general rely heavily on the senses of smell, hearing, taste, and touch, and less on the sense of sight. Like other traits, sense organs in a particular breed have been developed through selective breeding and domestication.

The Nose

The sense of smell is very important to Goldens. This sense enables them to find food and mates, and to decipher territories. Because Goldens have long been bred as hunting dogs, their highly developed sense of smell enables them to track game expertly.

The area of the olfactory system concerned with smell is more than 40 times larger in Goldens than in humans; in addition, Goldens can remember thousands of odors and can associate them with the appropriate people, animals, places, and events. The ability to discriminate between odors makes Goldens valuable for police narcotic and bomb squads.

The Ears

Goldens also possess a highly developed sense of hearing, superior to that of humans. They hear a wider range of sounds, especially high-pitched frequencies, such as those emitted from a Galton whistle ("silent" dog whistle). Goldens hear sounds from a much greater distance than do humans. Their acute hearing is also important to their usefulness as hunting dogs.

The Eyes

Goldens' peripheral vision is much greater than that of humans; however, their eyes do not focus as sharply as do those of humans. As a result, their eyes are much more sensitive to motion, but they must rely more on smell and sound to interpret what they see.

As previously mentioned, Goldens lack body sensitivity. This is important for hunting dogs that must run through thick brush and cold marshes in all types of weather.

Like other dogs, Goldens possess other senses that we still do not understand completely. For example, they have an innate sense of navigation. We have all heard reports of dogs traveling hundreds of miles to return home to their masters.

From Puppy to Adult Dog

The most critical part of your Golden puppy's life begins when you remove him from his littermates. From his seventh week on, your puppy begins to develop a new relationship with you. At this age your puppy is very curious and mischievous, and he lacks training. He must learn the rules of your home, as well as to differentiate play from seriousness.

The Golden Pup

Even before you bring your puppy home, he will have tested his strength in mock fights with his littermates. This helps improve his motor skills. He will also have begun to test the rules through his interactions with his mother.

When you bring your puppy home, he will be exceptionally adaptable (physically and emotionally) and will learn readily. Therefore, do not hesitate to begin training him immediately.

By the time your puppy is 12 or 13 weeks old, he will be completely aware of both himself and your home. His greatest joy will be to share discoveries with you. He will begin to investigate everything, primarily with his teeth, for at this time he begins to lose his baby teeth and get his permanent ones. Make sure you

How Old Is My Golden?
Dog/Human Age Equivalents

Dog's Age	Human's Age	Dog's Age	Human's Age
2 months	14 months	7 years	49 years
3 months	3 years	8 years	56 years
6 months	6 years	9 years	63 years
8 months	10 years	10 years	65 years
12 months	17 years	11 years	71 years
18 months	21 years	12 years	75 years
2 years	25 years	13 years	80 years
3 years	30 years	14 years	84 years
4 years	36 years	15 years	87 years
5 years	40 years	16 years	89 years
6 years	42 years	17 years	95 years

give your puppy enough toys to chew on. Remember that your puppy is still very impressionable, so treat him with care. Teach him the basic rules of your house, but be sure to be consistent and to control your emotions.

The Adolescent Golden

As your puppy reaches sexual maturity, he will enter a stage equivalent to human adolescence. At seven to ten months old he will almost reach his adult size. His curiosity is now bold, assertive interest. He is much more comfortable with your lifestyle and feels he should be included in all your activities. By this time your Golden should know what you expect of him and how he should behave. However, he will naturally try to challenge you in order to improve his rank. When this happens, do not lose your temper. Just teach your Golden—calmly and firmly—that you are in charge. Doing so will lead your dog through his final stage of development.

The Mature Golden

Once your Golden reaches maturity, he probably will not undergo any major behavioral changes (with the exception of mating urges). Your consistency and evenness of temper in training your dog should now pay off in many years of companionship with a loving, devoted, trustworthy Golden Retriever.

Encounters in the Outside World

It is important to familiarize your Golden puppy with the ways of humans and other

animals. Introducing your dog to the outside world while he is still very young will make vacations or other trips with your Golden much more pleasant. Your dog will be much happier if he learns not to fear people or other dogs.

On occasion take your dog with you when you shop. Being exposed to strange places and people (as long as you accompany him) will help increase the puppy's confidence in himself and in you. Also take the dog on short auto trips. Gradually lengthen the trips until the puppy is used to traveling.

The Travel Crate

When you travel by car, keep your dog in a small crate to prevent him from getting in your way and to protect him from injury through sudden stops. If you cannot bring a crate, teach your dog to lie down on the back seat. Never let him ride with his head out the window, for he can get foreign matter in his eyes. When you leave your puppy in the car, always open the windows enough for proper ventilation, but not enough for the dog to jump out. Heat can build up in a car very rapidly, so always park in the shade. If you plan to be gone a long time, leave your dog at home.

Controlled Encounters

In addition, walk your puppy (on a leash) in areas where you will encounter other people and dogs. If you like, let your Golden play with other dogs. Restrain your puppy until the strange dog approaches him. If the two wag their tails and sniff each other's nose and tail, you may assume they like each other. Your Golden puppy will almost always wag his tail. You can remove your puppy's leash if you wish, but remain nearby in case you are needed.

Your Golden and a strange dog will almost always try to establish a ranking order. This may include playful frolicking in which one dog ends up lying on its back in a subordinate position. However, the dogs may fight if neither is willing to back down, so be prepared. If either dog tries to challenge the other by displaying a threatening posture or by growling, immediately remove your Golden from the area.

How Your Dog Affects You

Recently, scientists have begun to study the psychological and behavioral responses of people to companion animals. Owning and caring for a pet is an effective means of reducing stress. It is also beneficial for the elderly, as well as the physically and mentally handicapped. As the owner of a Golden Retriever, you will undoubtedly become emotionally attached to your dog. Do not think of this as strange, even if you find it embarrassing. Remember that it is only natural to become attached to a living being with whom you share a long-term emotional commitment— whether human or canine.

Sharing sport and adventure with your Golden will mean sharing happiness, excitement, and friendship. Be assured that your dog will also experience these feelings and will often attempt to express his gratitude. Your Golden will make you feel loved and appreciated. Whenever you return home, you will be greeted by a dog that is happy to see you and that missed you when you were gone.

Your Golden will always love you for yourself. Your wealth or social and professional success are not important to him. He gives his love unquestioningly and completely; what greater devotion can anyone demand?

International Kennel Clubs

American Kennel Club
260 Madison Avenue
New York, NY 10016
Website: *www.akc.org/library.htm*
E-mail: info@akc.org

Canadian Kennel Club
89 Skyway Avenue, Suite 100
Etobicoke, Ontario M9W 6R4
Canada
Website: *www.ckc.ca/*
E-mail: information@ckc.ca

Golden Retriever Club of America (GRCA)
c/o Secretary
P.O. Box 20434
Oklahoma City, OK 73156
Website: *www.grca.org/*
E-mail: secretary@grca.org

The Kennel Club
1-5 Clargis Street
Picadilly, London W1Y 8AB
United Kingdom
Website: *www.the-kennel-club.org.uk/*
E-mail: info@the-kennel-club.org.uk/

National Retrieving Club
5 Deblyn Lane
West Chester, PA 19382
Website: *www.working-retriever.com/nrc/*

Magazines

Dog Fancy Magazine
P.O. Box 6050
Mission Viejo, CA 92690
Website: *www.dogchannel.com/dfdc_portal.aspx*

Dogs Monthly
61 Great Whyte
Ramsey, Huntingdon, PE26 1HJ
United Kingdom
Website: *http://www.dogsmonthly.co.uk*

Useful Literature

Bauer, Nona Kilgore. *Golden Retrievers for Dummies.* Foster City, California. IDG Books, Worldwide (2000).

Bonham, Margret H. *The Complete Idiots Guide to Golden Retrievers.* New York, New York. Alpha Books.

Cairns, Julie. *The Golden Retriever: All That Glitters.* Hoboken, New Jersey. John Wiley and Sons, Inc. (1998).

Coile, D. Caroline. *The Golden Retriever Handbook.* Hauppauge, New York: Barron's Educational Series, Inc. (2000).

Dunbar, Ian. *The Essential Golden Retriever.* New York, New York. Howell Book House (1998).

Fox, Michael W. *Dog Body? Dog Mind: Exploring Canine Consciousness and Total Well Being.* Guilford, Connecticut. The Lyons Press (2007).

Malloy, Maryle. *The Golden Retriever: An Owners Survival Guide.* Irvine, California. Bowtie Press (2003).

Millan, Cesar and Melissa Jo Peltier. *Be The Pack Leader: Use Cesar's Way to Transform Your Life . . . and Your Dog.* New York, New York. Crown Publishing Group (2007).

Vanderbilt, Arthur. *Golden Days: Memories of a Golden Retriever.* Minocqua, Wisconsin. Willow Creek Press (1998).